APPALACHIAN HERITAGE

VOL. 44, NO. 1
WINTER 2016

ESTABLISHED IN 1973

PUBLISHED QUARTERLY
by Berea College
CPO 2166
205 N. Main Street
Berea, KY, 40404

www.appalachianheritage.net

 Periodicals postage paid at Berea, Kentucky, and at additional mailing offices. ISSN# 03632318.

Electronic submissions only at www.appalachianheritage.net

Distributed by the University of North Carolina Press. Basic subscription price: $30/year for individuals, $40/year for institutions. For subscription requests and inquiries, visit the magazine's website, email uncpress_journals@unc.edu, or call 919.962.4201.

CONTENTS

EDITOR'S NOTE .... *Jason Howard* 5

2015 DENNY C. PLATTNER AWARDS 8

FICTION

What Lies on the Mind .... *Jeremy S. McQueen* 10

Pilgrims .... *Devin Murphy* 96

CREATIVE NONFICTION

Geographies of Pluto .... *Amelia Fowler* 32

A Queen in My Blue Jeans .... *Tessa McCoy* 85

POETRY

Caribou on a Slab of Plywood in Our Garden .. *Carol Hobbs* 30

Her Days .... *Carol Hobbs* 31

Laundry Woman .... *Kathleen Driskell* 42

What I Learned in My Mother's Kitchen .... *Kathleen Driskell* 43

Evolution .... *Kathleen Driskell* 44

Fish .... *Richard Hague* 60

Crow .... *Paul Nelson* 82

Winter's Raven .... *Paul Nelson* 84

When Those Days Come .... *Terry Ann Thaxton* 93

Nativity Scene on the Courthouse Lawn .... *Ryan Harper* 94

In My Window .... *Lydia Copeland Gwyn* 110

Power Outage .... *Ace Boggess* 112

To Know a Man Truly .... *Noel Smith* 120

Keepsake .... *Noel Smith* 121

INTERVIEW
Kathleen Driskell .... *Jason Howard* 47

CRAFT ESSAY
Bless Its Heart: The Irony of Appalachian Literature
.... *Maurice Manning* 61

BOOK REVIEWS
Mot: A Memoir (Einstein) .... *Greta McDonough* 113
Walk Till the Dogs Get Mean: Meditations on the Forbidden from Contemporary Appalachia (Blevins & McElmurray, eds.)
.... *Beth Newberry* 116

CONTRIBUTORS 124

COVER PHOTOGRAPH
Finch in Winter .... *Jennifer Even Melton*

EDITOR'S NOTE

JASON HOWARD

This January, the arts community in Kentucky had a close shave. Rumors were rife that Matt Bevin, the Commonwealth's new governor, was planning to propose abolishing the Kentucky Arts Council in his budget. Such a move would have been disastrous for artists and arts lovers alike: in 2015, the state agency awarded $3.3 million in grants to artists, schools, libraries, and community and arts organizations across Kentucky.

For Kentucky artists, the agency has long been a source of pride, not only for the financial support and creative validation that it has provided since its founding in 1966, but also for the simple fact that its work and presence has always pushed back against the nasty stereotype that the Commonwealth is filled with illiterate nabobs who don't know *Lady Chatterley's Lover* from Lady Antebellum. Its very presence sends the message that Kentucky arts and artists are to be valued. So it was not surprising when the arts community reacted swiftly and with collective fury, flooding social media and generating scores of telephone calls and emails to the governor and state legislators.

When the governor's budget was released, the arts council was ultimately spared. Instead, the Tourism, Arts and Heritage Cabinet, the council's parent agency—along with other cabinet departments—would be subjected to a nine percent cut and tasked with deciding how to distribute those reductions. Many arts advocates across the Commonwealth breathed a sigh of relief, murmuring that it might have been worse. And indeed it might have been. But aside from the issue of funding, the incident raised the serious question of how much the arts—and on a literary level, stories themselves—are valued.

"We tell ourselves stories in order to live," Joan Didion once wrote, a statement that if not quite literally true for many Kentuckians, Appalachians, and others across the country, comes pretty close. Storytelling has long been at the heart of our culture, an act of creativity that has sustained families in both good times and bad. On front porches in the cool of the day, over casseroles following a funeral, in the wake of epic floods, coal mining disasters, and deep poverty, the people of this region have always relied on the power of the narrative to communicate, commemorate, preserve and heal.

Appalachian Heritage was founded in 1973 in part to honor this tradition, and this issue in particular illustrates that focus, beginning with the winners of the 2015 Denny C. Plattner Awards. As you thumb through these pages, you'll see how tragedy impacts a community and its residents in Jeremy S. McQueen's story "What Lies on the Mind." You'll marvel at the honesty and vulnerability in Tessa McCoy's essay "A Queen in My Blue Jeans." You'll be moved as the narrator of Kathleen Driskell's poem "Laundry Woman" recalls her great-grandmother's life in service "to feed / her fatherless children." And you'll want to read Maurice Manning's craft essay "Bless Its Heart: The Irony of Appalachian Literature"—delivered as a keynote at Berea College's recent Appalachian Symposium—more than once to savor its eloquence and intellectual heft.

In his essay, Manning calls on us to "go forth and trust that the human imagination, wherever it resides, will call to life the things that matter." By doing so, we will also recommit ourselves to valuing story in both our individual lives and communities at large. ■

2015 DENNY C. PLATTNER AWARDS

The annual Plattner Awards were established in 1995 by Kenneth and Elissa Plattner to honor their late son and his love of writing. The awards are given to the finest pieces of fiction, creative nonfiction, and poetry that appeared in *Appalachian Heritage* during the previous year. Winners receive a $200 prize, and both winners and honorable mentions are awarded a handsome cherry wooden book rack designed and manufactured by Berea College Crafts.

FICTION

Judged by Silas House, author of A Parchment of Leaves *and* The Coal Tattoo

Winner: Clarissa Nemeth, "Broke Your Heart Just About Every Way How"

Honorable Mention: Natalie Sypolt, "Stalking the White Deer"

CREATIVE NONFICTION

Judged by Jeremy B. Jones, author of Bearwallow: A Personal History of a Mountain Homeland

Winner: Jackson Connor, "Speaking of Lineage"

Honorable Mention: Jessie van Eerden, "The Long Weeping"

POETRY

Judged by Jesse Graves, author of Basin Ghosts *and* Tennessee Landscape with Blighted Pine

Winner: Marianne Worthington, "I saw Bobby Bare kiss Marty Stuart"

Honorable Mention: Bill King, "Hawks at Dusk"

WHAT LIES
ON THE MIND

JEREMY S. MCQUEEN

The fog rose off the lake like puffs of smoke blown into the atmosphere. Heavy drops beat down the humidity that tried to creep up from the soil. It didn't have much of a fighting chance. Autumn gave up on its lie of better days to come with each dying leaf.

The breeze was dank against his skin, the bones in his knuckles aching from the morning dampness. His momma had been able to predict rainfall with an uncanny certainty. “Rain’s a comin,” she’d say, never blinking as she rubbed her hands together, like she was trying to scrub off the years’ worth of calluses. “My arthritis is startin’ to act up. It’ll be here for long, you watch and see.” It wouldn’t take a half hour before the Lord would prove her right.

He stood on the wraparound porch, overlooking the dock he’d built with his bare hands and the shimmering paleness that stretched for hundreds of acres through the evergreens and around the crooks and bends in the protected woodland, named after Daniel Boone. The warm cotton from his uniform pants and long shirtsleeves, coupled with the steam rising off black coffee, made quiet times on the back porch cherished gems in the rough of his days.

Thunder broke through the rain and fog like an angry voice from the past, tired of letting him have his hour of peace. He didn’t bother to jump at the sound. He’d expected as much to come sooner or later, as if his momma was whispering a countdown in the back of his head.

He didn’t budge from the banister when the phone rang in the cabin. This was his time to think before whatever hell waited for him outside opened its arms to show him its handiwork for the day. Besides, he knew that a call this early wouldn’t be any good, and there was no sense in wasting any time with the awkwardness of one of his deputies trying to search for the right words to explain what had happened. He figured they could break the news quicker to a machine.

The answering service clicked on, and his wife’s voice started to recite the message she’d recorded years ago. “Hello, you’ve gotten caught in the Webb’s answering machine. We’re sorry to say that we’re not available right now. Please leave your name and number, and we’ll try to free you as soon as we can.”

He wasn't a damn bit sorry for not being available, but his ears perked up anyhow to listen to whoever was aimed at pestering him at this morning hour.

"Uh, hey Sheriff Webb—this is your deputy—Jamie. We've got a car accident over on Highway 25—close to your place, I reckon. The car's wrecked up pretty bad. Head toward town and you'll find it. Anyway, I'm headed over there now. I guess I'll see you at the scene, boss."

The Sheriff threw back the last gulp from his mug while it was still close to hot. He held the coffee in his mouth for a few seconds while he stared out at the mist and the clouds and the darkness hanging over the speckled lake. He shook his head and turned toward the screen door.

He moved through the house as if he was a stranger to its way of life, only stopping at the places where he knew there was something of his to take. He grabbed his keys from the wooden table in the hallway, and fetched his raincoat and Clover County Sheriff's Department cap from the coat rack beside the front door. Once he had these items, he turned to look at the lonely cabin behind him—a place that missed all the livelier parts of a life that no longer existed.

Sheriff Webb climbed into his Ford Crown Vic and looked over at his little Ranger pickup. There was a twinge of sadness that leapt up inside his throat every time he was called away from it—not because of what it was, but more likely what it represented. The pickup had known all the better times that he remembered. The youngest part of him felt sorry that his old friend had to stay home and endure the loneliness alone.

The cruiser rolled over the dirt and grass of the yard until the four rubbers crunched onto the gravel. The rock path snaked and arched through the woods of the holler until the nose of the Ford peeked its headlights onto the winding blacktop of the main roadway. Sheriff Webb stopped at the intersection, thinking about what he might find at the bend up ahead.

Once he straightened the car onto 25, his eyes drifted past the fields near the roadside, where the grass looked as if it had a few drops of life remaining in the dirt below. The faded green reminded him of the apron Jean liked to wear when she tended her garden—the emerald dye had bled out over the decades of repeated washings. He hadn't had the energy to keep up what she'd planted this year—just another way he'd failed her as a husband, and as a man.

The Sheriff settled his gaze upon the hills at the ridgeline, the maples and oaks showing off their burnt oranges and fiery reds, pieces of the dying sprinkled over the last of the living. Both his wife and daughter had been born in the fall, and he figured that explained their love for the season. He'd always thought pumpkin pies and turkey salad were the only good in these months—but that was only because Jean and Marilyn had made both of those things.

The faded green reminded him of the apron Jean liked to wear when she tended her garden—the emerald dye had bled out over the decades of repeated washings.

Every phone call that rang into the office, or to his home, made him fear the worst. His mind wanted to always ready him for the looming truth that his baby girl was gone and she wouldn't be coming back. Marilyn had forever been wild and free, but she loved him and her mother more than anything else he knew about. She never would've just left without as much as a note as to where she was headed. But that's what had happened and he couldn't explain it.

He knew that Marilyn leaving had something to do with her husband. That seems to always be the case. Just as the lack of sunlight and the cold kills most of the leaves in the trees, he was sure that Bill Sexton Jr. was the cause behind his daughter's disappearance. Jean thought as much, too. Once the idea had taken root in her brain, it was a thought that couldn't be dug out without damaging the nerve endings. He reckoned that's what brought on the aneurysm.

The car crash didn't take long to sneak up on him. The flashing lights from the police cruisers caught his eyes first, like the bright beacons the carnies used to lure all the country kids out of the woods during the county fair. Somehow he had to remind himself that those red and blue spinners didn't go with happy. He didn't hear the ambulance sirens yet, so maybe he had time. His deputies had already taped off the space where the vehicles had gone off the pavement.

From the looks of things, he knew that one of the cars had forced the other into the embankment against its will. Such truths end up being evident after one has seen them enough. He pulled his Ford behind the other two cruisers and cut off the engine. He could already smell the burnt rubber and smoke, as thick as the rain clouds overhead, and flooding the interior of his Crown Vic. He imagined it to smell like Los Angeles smog, but he couldn't be sure.

When the Sheriff wandered over to the mess of metal that lay in the mud with the wet leaves, he could hear his deputies, Jamie and Boyd, chatting while they circled the wrecked vehicles. A black Ranger pickup sat with its nose planted in the hillside like it was growing there, and a white Chevy S-10 turned over next to it—the side of its bed crumpled.

"Did you watch the Kentucky game last night?" Jamie asked, shining his flashlight inside the black pickup. Boyd did the same thing on the passenger's side of the truck.

"Nah—I didn't reckon there was much to watch this year. How'd they do?"

"Not bad, actually. They got a couple homegrown boys this season to go along with some of their upperclassmen. If Tubby can manage them, they might get back to the Final Four."

"They still got that boy from out in California—Compton, I think it was?"

"Yep, he had a hell of a game last night. I mean—they weren't playing nobody worth bragging about, but he had a double-double by halftime. He had over twenty at the final buzzer."

"They're gonna need him to put up those kind of numbers every game, if they're gonna have a chance. My brother played with that California kid at a basketball camp. He said he caught the ball on a fast break and jumped over top a high school boy that tried to take a charge."

"You two gonna tell me what the hell happened here, or should I wait for the play-by-play from Monday Night Football, too?" Sheriff Webb asked, staring daggers at his deputies.

"Oh shit—sorry, boss," Jamie said, whipping around from the driver window.

"Sorry, Sheriff," Boyd echoed, walking around the back end of the open tailgate. "Driver of this here pickup is deader than a doornail. He was gone before we got here. We were just checking for dope or booze until the medical team pulls him outta that cab."

"And where is the ambulance, exactly? It has been called, right? A passerby rubber neckin' usually gets it called in before we even have a chance to pick up the phone."

"Yes sir, it's been called in," Jamie confirmed. "Both of the ambulances were already out this morning on two other car wrecks. A woman on the Owsley line had some bad luck—hit two deer, and a man over close to Clay County fell asleep at the wheel and drove into a creek bed."

"Who's inside this one? I don't think I knowed of another black Ranger in the county."

"Just a youngun, Sheriff—Nathan Isaacs. He was a senior—worked at Bob Sexton's gas station. I don't guess he had the pickup very long. I've only seen him driving it a few times."

"That's a terrible shame. He came from a good family. His daddy pastors a church over in East Bernstadt, I reckon. I've knowed his folks since we were younguns ourselves. I hate to have to lay this kind of grief on their hearts. They sure won't forgive me for it any time soon."

"I guess you can guess whose S-10 that is," Jamie said, nodding to the white pickup lying up on its passenger side. "You have to hand it to him—he knows how to find trouble."

"That Harold's truck?" the Sheriff asked, knowing the answer. Jamie and Boyd nodded back at him. He sighed and shook his head at their confirmation. "Where is he? Is he alright?"

"He looks no worse than usual, Sheriff," Boyd replied. "He might have a concussion. He says he needs to speak with you in private—about matters not meant for our ears."

On the other side of the police cruisers, sitting closer to the highway than most men would feel comfortable with, sat Harold Collins, squatted like a youngun in kindergarten class, legs tucked up under his tail. When Sheriff Webb got closer to the man next to the road, Harold's eyes popped open like a tripwire had been snagged by the Sheriff's britches leg. This stopped Sheriff Webb in his own tracks, and he looked Harold over with more caution than care.

"You okay, Harold?" he asked, looking him up and down. "Anything broken?"

"I'll live, Ansil," he answered, keeping his stare fixed. "I shouldn't have lived, God Almighty knows that better than anyone—the way that boy was driving. He came around that curve like a bat out of Hell—never even braked once as far as I could tell. I'm lucky he hit the truck bed instead of my driver door, or you and I wouldn't be having this talk now."

"I have to ask, Harold. Have you been drinkin'? You know how this is gonna look."

"Ansil—you know there ain't many a day that goes by without me taking a drink. But, as it happens, I ran out last night, and I woke up with a craving for some biscuits and gravy. I was on my way over to Marlene's Place to get me a bite to eat when Evil Knievel knocked me over."

"My deputies say you wanted to talk to me in private? Well—here I am. What was so important you couldn't tell them?" Harold blinked twice and lowered his chin to his chest.

"When his pickup hit me, I thought it was gonna blow us both to smithereens. But my S-10 spun sideways and tilted. My seatbelt held me behind the wheel. I knew how hard he must've hit the bank after plowing through me. I climbed out and got to him as quick as I could. He wasn't making any sense, Ansil—death was all over him—gargling with brain trauma."

"Harold—are you sayin' that boy was alive when you found him? Did he say any final goodbyes to his folks or anything? Speak as straight as you can to me now."

"Dammit, Ansil—I'm speaking as plain as white bread. Yes—the boy was alive. But he didn't say goodbye. What he did mumble—between gurgles and slurring—was simple. 'Tell Sheriff Webb—it was Bill Jr. I saw him dump them.' The Lord took him after that breath."

■ ■ ■

Sheriff Webb sat alone in his Crown Vic, his eyes carving out holes in his dashboard like mice nibbling away at all the plastic between them and anything real. He thought about

Harold's voice and Nathan Isaacs' words over and over again—words that were uttered in a dying breath. He reckoned that anything worth saying with death sitting beside you ought to be worth saying. Nathan could've said anything in that moment, but he chose to pass on a message instead.

The medics were loading Nathan's body inside the ambulance when Harold started to ease down into the back of Boyd's cruiser. He'd passed a Breathalyzer blow—maybe the first time since he and the Sheriff had been younguns. Boyd offered to give him a free ride to the hospital, and he'd accepted as long as Boyd would take him to get some biscuits and gravy afterwards. Harold turned and nodded at the Sheriff one last time before he ducked inside.

He turned away from Jamie at that point and took a few steps toward the painted lines on the highway like he might keep on walking plumb across the county.

When both the ambulance and Boyd had driven off, he got out of the police car and approached Jamie, who was still piddling around the wreckage—taking photos and notes.

"So, what did crazy ole Harold have to say?" Jamie asked, as the Sheriff got nearer. Sheriff Webb shook his head and spit a mouthful of tobacco juice into the weeds at the ditch.

"Son—there ain't one crazy bone in Harold Collins' body. He's a professional drunk—I reckon he's been that ever since comin' back from the war. That don't make him a bit crazy."

"Sorry, boss. I didn't know Harold was a veteran. Where did he serve?"

"There's books full of things you don't know, Jamie. Harold and I grew up together—back when the coal and lumber companies owned anything worth mentionin' in this county. We both served in Korea and we lived to tell about it. Sometimes I reckon Harold wishes he didn't come back home a'tall. Jim Beam and the prison are the only company he's kept for fifty years."

"Well—you think this here was just an accident? We'll do a tox screening on Nathan, but we didn't find any obvious evidence in the truck—not even rolling papers or a pill bottle."

"The way Harold tells it—Nathan didn't even bother slowin' up. His story seems to match the lack of skid marks on the asphalt. Have that Ranger towed to a garage outside the county and inspected for any foul play. You give me the word as soon as you know somethin'."

"10-4, boss—will do. Whatta you gonna do with the rest of your morning?"

"Well, for starters, I have to drive over to Sharon and Donnie's home. This mornin' will likely be the last time I'm welcome to pay them a visit for a good while."

He turned away from Jamie at that point and took a few steps toward the painted lines on the highway like he might keep on walking plumb across the county. As soon as his Red Wings felt a few pebbles beneath them, he stopped and looked over his shoulder at his deputy.

"Say—tell me somethin', son. If you got wind that someone had dumped a body, and the informant didn't tell you where, what would be your best guess?" To his surprise, Jamie didn't take more than a few seconds to think about it. He sat his camera and notepad down on the open tailgate and jammed his plump hands down into his brown uniform pants.

"Well, boss—dump sounds like water to me, if we're talking about bodies. Where else would any criminal mastermind think the law wouldn't find their wrongdoings? I can't speak for you or Boyd, but I don't go swimming very often. How come you ask? Are we missing a body?"

"I just had evil on my mind, son. There's been too much bad goin' on lately—those McElroy folks gettin' burnt up last summer; my Marilyn been missin' now since not long after that fire; Jean's passin'; and now this Isaacs boy runnin' off the road for no good reason."

"Maybe it's the change of the times, sir—the new millennium and everything. But—as far as dumping bodies goes—there's only one place in Clover deep enough for that kind of behavior, and your cabin sits right next to it. Who would have such gumption to take a chance?"

"I don't reckon that anyone desperate enough would be scared off on account of me livin' next door to the only lake in the county, son. Surely you've seen enough stupid movies to know better. Besides, there are a few other entry points I can think of right off top of my head."

"Well—even so—there ain't too many places in the lake deep enough that anybody would trust a corpse to not float back into the daylight. You'd have to be near retarded."

"Or—like I said before—desperate, young man. You add that with a little cockiness, and you're bound to find yourself more than a handful of common criminals. You get to movin' on that pickup inspection. Let me know as soon as you get word of anything of interest."

Sheriff Webb slid down in the Ford cruiser and didn't waste any time firing the engine back to life. It hummed like the inside of the Sheriff's brain, which was full of thoughts he wanted to shout to the wind. He was angry and curious and sad—all at the same time. Was there any truth in Nathan Isaacs' final words? Why would a boy have a lie on his mind before he was about to meet his maker? He didn't find it sensible to put too much stock in coincidences.

The cruiser's wheels gripped the grooves on the roadway like bubble gum on the high school sidewalk. Sheriff Webb pushed his boot harder into the accelerator, climbing each small hump in the pavement and lifting his foot to coast into each dip, riding the momentum around the never-ending curves between Nathan's Ford Ranger and his folks' place up on Coyote Creek.

His eyes darted from side-to-side, peering into the lightening clouds that hung over top of the mountains as if they were canvas drapes, becoming more transparent as the day unfolded. His jawbone was sore, and when he brought his hand to the side of his cheek, he realized that he was gritting his molars into a fury against one another. Only his less-than-Christian son-in-law could provoke such mindless anger, and he wished he had more than the words of a dead boy.

Bill Sexton Jr. had always been a rich man, and as best as he could figure, that's all Marilyn ever saw in him. The Sexton family had made their fortune during the Depression, buying and renting all the land and real estate in the county. Only a small piece of the population had been able to afford their own property, and the Sextons preyed on the rest. He could even remember his own family renting from Bill Sr.—before the war and before they built their cabin.

Both Bill Jr. and his brother, Bobby, had been as ruthless as their father ever since they were big enough to wipe their own asses. Bobby went into private business and opened his own full-service gas station. He eventually ran off most of his competitors when he started lending credit to God and everybody under the sun. The wealth and freedom was enough for Bobby.

Bill Jr. wasn't satisfied with all the money he inherited from his daddy's sins. He went to college and became an elementary teacher just for show. Marilyn always spoke to him and Jean about Bill Jr.'s aspirations, and how he was aiming his sights higher than school administration. It didn't take him longer than a few years as a glorified nanny before he used his money to get elected as superintendent. Marilyn disappeared not long after.

Sheriff Webb pulled onto the busted blacktop that ran parallel to Coyote Creek, and slowed his speed to not much more than a cruise. He knew the Isaacs lived at the end of the holler and there were about thirty houses and trailers between the mouth and the five miles that stretched to the mountain bank, each sheltering any number of pre-school younguns itching to scratch a wild hair and run out in the middle of the road. The thought made him slow to a crawl.

Sharon and Donnie's white house sat at the end of the narrow cul de sac like a pristine government dwelling compared to most of its neighbors, who actually did rely on federal funds to keep the lights on. Donnie was a good man, but you could make the argument that he'd provided for his family with the prayers of others—most of which lived in his neck of the woods. Their older son was off at a Bible college in North Carolina, learning the family business.

The Ford whistled its arrival like a braking train when it pulled to a stop on the short concrete driveway—gears squeaking as it parked beside the Isaacs' chain-link fence that encased their half-acre of yard. When Sheriff Webb stood up beside his open door, Donnie already waited on the porch, his hands resting inside his blue jeans. He waved his hand like there were hundreds of miles between him and the police car, wondering if he could be seen.

"Hidy, Sheriff," he called from their black, wrought iron door. "Your deputy said we could be expecting you. You just missed him on the phone. He said he'd call back."

"Well—that'll be fine. How are you, Donnie? Everything alright at the church?"

"Oh, just fine and dandy—plenty of good people gathers to worship every Wednesday and Sunday. Lot of good folks in this holler makes the trip. We sure wouldn't mind seeing you there anytime, Sheriff. We'd be honored to have you join us in fellowship whenever the spirit calls you." The Sheriff spat the jawful of tobacco into the weeds, before biting his bottom lip.

"Thank ye for the offer, Donnie. I'll give it some thought. I guess Jamie was the one that gave you a call, was it?" He looked careful across the yard to see what Donnie knew.

"Yeah, I reckon so. He said to tell you he took the pickup to Laurel County. He said he'd have more information for you soon. You want to come over here and have a seat? We got fresh coffee brewing inside. Sharon made a delicious pound cake last night. That sound good to you?"

He lifted the metal latch on the fence and stepped through the gateway onto the sidewalk made from creek rocks.

"Well—I don't reckon I should stay too long. I've got other business to tend to today."

"Aw, nonsense. At least have a cup of Joe. Sharon—Sheriff Webb's here. Bring him a cup of coffee, honey. Don't mind that gate, Sheriff. Come on over here and sit down."

He lifted the metal latch on the fence and stepped through the gateway onto the sidewalk made from creek rocks. He watched his feet as he took clean steps to avoid snagging his soles on one of the jagged edges sticking out of the concrete holding the family of stones together. He sat down on one of the patio chairs facing Donnie, reluctant to look him square in the eyes.

The iron frame opened and Sharon backed her way through the doorway. "Here you go, Sheriff. Do you take cream or sugar with your coffee?" He shook his head and tried to smile.

"No, ma'am. I like my coffee as black as the night—always have, I reckon. I can't start addin' sugar to everything at my age. I'll have the diabetes quicker than lightnin' can flash."

"I thought you'd be a black coffee man. Let me know if it's not strong enough for you." He took a careful sip from the mug and the bitterness reminded him of his mission.

"Thank ye for your hospitality, Donnie. Sorry that I didn't give you any notice."

"Don't you worry about it. I'm surprised you had the time to stop by so early. The scanner sure has been busy with those car accidents this morning. This foggy weather might be the worst for anyone getting out on the road—just short of the snow and ice waiting for us."

He could feel his face tighten where all the lines met one another, and his heart pounded at his chest like a bass drum at a Friday night football game over in London. He waited for the hot liquid to warm his vocal chords, as he searched his mind for how to deliver the awful news.

"That coffee doing the trick, Sheriff?" Sharon asked. She smiled at his distant nod.

"What did you folks hear on the scanner about the car accidents?"

"Oh, nothing much—just the usual facts. One told the make and model of the vehicle that hit the deer over close to Owsley. The last one that came on said there was a fatality—"

Sheriff Webb watched Donnie's eyes change, his brow drooping to reveal he suspected something that hadn't been as clear to him before the sun shone on it at just the right angle.

"Just why are you here, Sheriff?" he asked, swallowing a dry gasp of air. He reached over to take Sharon's hand, and she looked at him with a confused stare like she didn't understand why he was being so forward in front of company. Pinkness rose to her cheeks and she smiled.

“I’m sorry for not being forthright with you folks. I’m sorry for accepting the invitation to your porch to drink your coffee. The truth is—” Sheriff Webb paused and sat the half-full mug on the iron table. He clasped his hands together like he’d seen his momma do so many times when he was a younger man. His hand reached up to remove his cap and he bowed his head.

“The truth is—I’ve come here today on official business as your Sheriff, and as your neighbor. I’m sorry to tell you that your son, Nathan, passed on this mornin’. His Ranger hit another truck’s bed and plowed into an embankment. I can’t tell you how sorry I am to say this.”

Sharon didn’t say anything. Her face shriveled and her lips curled. Donnie’s eyes got as soggy as the ground beneath the porch. He pulled his wife close to him and squeezed her tight while they whimpered and held one another. The cordless phone began beeping on the table. Neither of them moved to answer it, so he took it upon himself to usher the phone away.

“Isaacs residence,” he answered, walking down from the porch steps.

“Sheriff Webb—this is Jamie. I’m still in London with the pickup. The inspection ain’t finished yet, but there was an easy find. You’re never gonna believe this, Sheriff. Nathan Isaacs’ brake lines were cut—sliced in half like chopped spaghetti. I’d say Nathan had an enemy.”

■ ■ ■

He’d been sitting on his son-in-law’s front porch for nearly two hours when his eyes caught the first glimmer of light that must’ve reflected off one of the many pieces of chrome that adorned the Ford F-250. It slowed at the end of the quarter-mile, blacktop driveway, and he knew that the driver could look across the open field and see him sitting there, rocking back and forth like he was just waiting to catch up and talk about old times.

He followed the rumbling truck with his eyes as it climbed the gradual incline over the little bumps in the pasture. The shiny fiberglass looked as blue as the uniforms the Wildcats wore on the television for away games. He reckoned that Bill Jr. probably paid more for the special paint job—no more than a drop in the bucket compared to what he's worth. One of the four garage doors opened—the one near the house—and the truck moseyed inside.

Bill Jr. walked outside onto his driveway through the open door and he kept it raised. He gazed across the field like he was examining the growth of a pretend crop. Then he hacked up something from deep in his thick throat and let it drip out of his jiggling jaws onto the grass.

Bill Jr. let his suit jacket fall off his broad shoulders, exposing the wet spots under his arms and at the place where the Sheriff guess his navel would probably be...

"I didn't expect to see you today, Ansil. And what do I owe the pleasure?"

Bill Jr. let his suit jacket fall off his broad shoulders, exposing the wet spots under his arms and at the place where the Sheriff guessed his navel would probably be—like a tiny hole in the middle of a giant doughnut that always tried to protrude through the buttons of his shirts. The Sheriff unscrewed the lid from a plastic Coke bottle and spat a stream of brown juice inside.

"Why do you reckon grown men lie, Bill Jr.? I s'ppose we've all got our own reasons for not bein' honest with ourselves. When I wake up in the mornin' and understand that I've lived through another night—to face another nightmare of a day without my Jean, or without my baby girl—I choose to tell myself the lie that this might be the day that one of them comes back to me." The Sheriff looked over at his son-in-law. "What lies do you tell yourself?"

Bill Jr. chuckled enough to make the fat at his neck shake like Jell-O. "I don't rightly know what you're really asking, Ansil. I try not to dabble in lies, whether I'm thinking out loud, or sharing a conversation with fine Christian folks like yourself. What's this all about?"

"You heard from my daughter, Bill Jr.?" he asked, leaning forward in the rocking chair to stop its back-and-forth motion. He sat his Coke bottle down and shifted the ball of tobacco to his other cheek. Bill Jr. laid his jacket on the porch banister and pulled his britches higher.

"No, I haven't. You know I'd tell you if I'd heard a whisper of news about Marilyn."

"Uh-huh—of course you would. I know that's likely true. Problem is—I'm a bit concerned about whether we're ever gonna hear from her again. And I bet you'd shit your pants if you ever did hear from her. The dead don't make it a habit of carrying on conversations."

"Now what proof you have of saying something like that, Ansil? Jesus Christ, you worry me sometimes old man. You need to get that idea out of your head. Marilyn left me, too."

"Don't blaspheme, Bill Jr. You're gonna need all the brownie points you can buy with the Lord above. We got an interestin' tip—said they saw you dump somethin' big in the lake." He saw a change flicker in Bill Jr.'s eyes like sharp steel at sunset, fearing what he didn't know.

"The funny thing is—that tip was given to us by a youngun with his final breath of life. He died this mornin' when his truck wouldn't stop. We found out later that his brake lines had been severed. Who would do such a thing, you wonder? Must've been coverin' a lie."

"I wouldn't know, Ansil. I don't have a damn thing to hide, much less from you."

"I'm glad to hear you say that, Bill Jr. Judge Peters was kind enough to grant me a warrant to search your property—considering the circumstances. We're also gonna drag the lake. You and I both know there ain't but a handful of deep spots. It shouldn't take us more than a few days to find what we're after. You could save us all the time and trouble, and spit out the truth."

"That's too bad about the boy, but you're not going to find anything at the bottom of that lake I'm responsible for, Ansil. As for my property, knock yourself out. There's plenty to search. You should've brought along a small army to help you canvass this farm."

"You might be right about that. But, I figured I'd just start fishin' in your truck box and go from there. You see—any man that's got a mind to cut someone's brake lines probably don't have the mind to clean their tools real nice before they show up for a day of work at the office."

Sheriff Webb rose to his feet and stepped off the porch. He handed the folded piece of paper to his daughter's husband, and walked past his round outline. He hadn't made it out of the yard before Bill Jr.'s hands wrapped around his throat like two boxing gloves on a banana.

"I'll give you something to look for old man," Bill Jr. whispered in his ear. "I'll teach you what you get for snooping in places where your goddamn nose don't belong."

Two gunshots ricocheted off the hillsides like firecrackers in a cave. He felt Bill Jr.'s grip loosen and his weight collapse behind him. The heavy man lay on his side, clutching his legs and grimacing as if he'd been stung by a couple bees. His khaki pants showed crimson at the knees.

The Sheriff looked down at Bill Jr. for a moment, and then he raised his eyes to Harold Collins and gave him a nod. He turned toward the blue pickup and didn't stop until he was at the toolbox behind the cab window. He put on two latex gloves and opened the lid to rummage through the steel container. His heart sank when he pulled the bolt cutters from the darkness. ■

CARIBOU ON A SLAB OF PLYWOOD IN OUR GARDEN

My father says they are so pretty, caribou. And they are.
I smooth one's head around the muzzle, splay of white
above the mouth, back toward the soft cheek.
The caribou's eyes are open so I sing to it
hush-a-bye, don't you cry
I have a pretty voice. My father hums along,
and cuts away the skin from the severed hind quarter,
or rather cuts, then lifts the skin back as if he were helping
a woman remove her coat when she's come in from the
cold.

CAROL HOBBS

HER DAYS

When I was a girl I knew
leaving me was in her.
I dressed up the stage of my mother's story.
I could have charged quarters for that
privilege. I am telling
the truth. She was such composition.
Sunday, hat and gloves, my brother's baby curl tucked
into her bible, Leviticus, a photo of gladiolas; Monday,
a line of laundry hung in perfect graduation, and so on.
Every supper preordained: chicken soup on Wednesdays,
Fridays, salt fish in drawn butter.
A child wants to believe what she's told,
not what she glimpses in the two step swing of days—
every well-thumbed letter from my aunt,
postmarks Germany, Cyprus, Ontario, saved
in a blue flowered suitcase. She'd slip
sometimes, let supper burn
while she read novels. And sometimes
she'd let me dig to the bottom of her
drawstring handbag for spearmint gum and I'd take
my time, pull out her tortoiseshell comb, a gift
from a boy on a black Schwinn bike, long before
any of this. She wanted to have
what she wanted—a map with an evacuation route,
new vistas, books, what she didn't already know.

CAROL HOBBS

GEOGRAPHIES OF PLUTO

AMELIA FOWLER

We do not know the geography of Pluto as intimately as those celestial bodies closer to Earth. Looking up, one eye closed, I could trace the Moon's *Mare Serenitatis* with my pinky finger as if grazing the dark circles under a lover's eyes. The lunar maria, plains of basalt astronomers once mistook for oceans, do not amaze the human eye. We know, too, the landscape of Mars: a cratered planet tinted red with iron oxide. And there is Jupiter's constant, red storm; the metallic frost of a Venusian winter. Earth itself we have the taste of, the rich denseness having found its way into our mouths as young children. Pluto is a dead, solid body—resistant to study, sovereign of its cold corner of space.

■ ■ ■

Death is cosmic, universal; even stars die—a dark inward collapse we do not understand. The universe itself will die, stretched thin and cold.

Cemeteries lie beside the roads of West Virginia, common as roadkill. Some are gated and manicured, have names like God's Acre or Spring Hill; a sign reads *Closed at Dusk*. Others seem less cemetery than graveyard, wild and untended: swallowed by woods, gravestones mouldering. My mother taught me to hold my breath driving past. We buried my tabby cat under a rotted crabapple tree in my parents' backyard, her grave marked by white garden fencing, unvisited.

■ ■ ■

My mother described death to me after my grandmother died: a heavenly vacuum sucks the spirit out of the chest cavity and the soul soars through the sky to meet God in Heaven, a place past the edge of the universe. Though five years old, I imagined my grandmother's soul, a trail of thick fog escaping Earth's atmosphere to wander the long, empty stretches between the stars and planets till it reached the bright white wall of Heaven. She had lost her human features—the false teeth, the gold watch, the parrot and poodle left behind. Bodiless, the female pronouns did not apply.

That was the last year my mother, father, and I still lived in the West Side Charleston apartment, a basement twobedroom with plastic covering the windows in winter and the occasional rat or mouse. The moon still followed my mother's Honda at night and I believed I could see an object hundreds of miles distant if only I did not look away.

■ ■ ■

The summer before kindergarten, we moved into a house at the center of what my mother called a good neighborhood, a tidy and hilly subdivision outside of Charleston. My parents divided the house into basement and first floor, father and mother—an arrangement born of necessity, as my father worked nights and my mother days, but sustained permanently by estrangement.

My mother's domain, the first floor, is bright and windowed, flooded with light during the day and at night dully illuminated by the neighbors' porch lights and the headlights of cars.

The smell of cleaner overwhelms—Pine Sol, lemon Pledge, Windex. My mother sleeps in the corner bedroom, alone between bleachwhite sheets.

My father's basement smells of cigarette smoke and slept-in clothes. Cat hair covers the armchair, the love seat. The tabby, devoted to my father, lived down there until she died in her sleep and was buried under the crabapple tree. Shrubberies and flowers dominate the few windows. My father's bed is made with old, floral sheets.

■ ■ ■

There is no life on Pluto, nor was there ever; it is a world resigned to silence and stillness. On Pluto, our Sun is only a bright pore in the sky's tight fabric—little more than a star among other stars, distant and cold and irrelevant. The dwarf planet is one of many objects littering the edge of our solar system within the icy Kuiper belt.

■ ■ ■

The year I turned seven, my mother miscarried early in a pregnancy and spent weeks sick behind the closed door of her bedroom—a blue room, its many windows curtained to keep the light out. She allowed only my father behind the door. Three years later, she gave birth to my brother, and I sometimes feel as if I imagined the shut door, the quiet.

There is no life on Pluto, nor was there ever; it is a world resigned to silence and stillness.

My mother prefers to bury bad memories. The few photographs I have seen of her family are unlabeled. The careful cursive of names and dates begins only after I am born—*Claire '91*, an infant in an Olan Mills portrait with my father, nearly purple with laughter; *Claire '93*, lying in the grass with a white cat.

■ ■ ■

My mother's father was a pedophile and an alcoholic; he sexually abused my mother and her siblings until he died the year she started seventh grade. This she told me in a phone conversation my senior year of college, the year I lived alone in a basement apartment in Morgantown. There is a school picture of my mother at twelve, labeled *Ruth Ann* in what must be my grandmother's backslanted handwriting—unreadable if you do not know to look for the specific slopes of my mother's name. Her face is pale, the nose long, eyes green and eager. The teacher has brushed her hair into pigtails, the babyfine strands tied in place with red yarn; my mother told me this, that it was the teacher and not her mother who combed her hair, when she found the photograph where I had hidden it in my dresser drawer.

■ ■ ■

We have a false familiarity with Pluto. A planet until 2006—before that, the small ninth planet past Neptune on classroom posters of the solar system, in science fair dioramas, and the *S* volume of the *World Book Encyclopedia*.

An eleven-year-old English schoolgirl named the planet for the god of the dead. The name distorts the distance between Pluto and Earth; the name can be studied, tasted and felt in the mouth as a common object. Until adulthood, I did not understand how little we know about Pluto, how its distance defies all but the bleariest photographs. Language is an incomplete power—nameless, Pluto would still be cold and far and alien. Pluto predates language, is far older than human consciousness.

■ ■ ■

My father's sadnesses resurface when he drinks. He misses his mother, the woman for whom I am named. He misses his many siblings who are alive but faraway and quiet, save for one sister who calls when she has been drinking. The weekends I am home, he says, "You know I love you, Claire," and I say, "I love you, too," but climb the stairs to my mother's floor where sadness is entombed, set apart.

■ ■ ■

One spring evening in third grade, my mother and I cut stars out of blue cardstock while my father drank a case of beer in the basement. With a thin paintbrush, we spread Elmer's Glue from the stars' centers to each coronal point. Now and then, my mother stopped painting to yell down the basement stairs to my father, "Corky, you sure you don't want me to heat you up something?" to which he replied, "No." My father often disappeared down the road in his truck after he had been drinking—those times he stayed put in the basement were a relief.

We sprinkled the stars with silver glitter and hung them with dental floss, taped the ends to the ceiling above my bed. Languid, they swayed in the air conditioning, their calm blue belying radiation and thermal fusion.

■ ■ ■

That year, my favorite book was *D'Aulaire's Book of Greek Myths,* a large, colorful book I refused to return to the school library. Its glossy sleeve had been covered in protective plastic by the librarian, and the spine crinkled in greeting each time I opened it. The binding, halfbroken by constant use, fell open to the best illustrations: the transformation of Acteon into a stag, his hunting hounds salivating; the ascent of Selene's crescent chariot above a nocturnal Greek countryside; and a landscape of the underworld. Tall poplars, the river Styx, the bent heads of the dead—sketched out in soft black pencil, framed by earth and an overhang of roots as if we, in the world of the living, only had to dig to discover this dark place.

■ ■ ■

My senior year of college, I lived alone in a basement apartment I could never get clean—dirt pressed the walls in. Most nights I spent in the bathtub, the place I felt cleanest, reading thin books of poetry.

It was quiet then, and if new snow had fallen during the night, mine would be the only footprints.

Once winter came, I took walks, too, down the small street where I lived, often at three or four in the morning. It was quiet then, and if new snow had fallen during the night, mine would be the only footprints. Past the mosque, past a house seemingly abandoned save for a lighted basement window, past the university Credit Union, past a motel with no cars in its snowthick lot. The street ended at the hospital parking lot, which stretched far and white and empty.

■ ■ ■

There are two kinds of winter nights. The winter night of snow still falling: the sky a false bright, dense snow clouds reflecting pink and orange city light, no chance of stars or moon. The snow falls thick, uncovered ears ache. And the winter night of snow fallen: the sky cleared, stars somehow more numerous. Silent and desolate, the Earth basks in old light. It is this second, exposed night that leaves me stricken. A Plutonian landscape, atmosphere thin, transparent. Outer space there, right there: that glassy, inhospitable womb of planets, stars, and dust.

It seems impossible that a rock as small as Pluto should have five moons: Charon, Styx, Nix, Kerberos, and Hydra. Names suggesting myth and the underworld, even monstrosity—consonant names fixed in hard lines. Charon is over half the size of Pluto itself, and the bodies are sometimes considered a pair: Hades and his ferryman.

■ ■ ■

That winter, a feral colony of cats took shelter under the stairs outside my bedroom window; at night, I heard them fighting and fucking, though I could not tell the difference. I was sleeping with an astrophysics major who wrote poetry; he was an alcoholic, deeply depressed when sober. Antidepressants softened his erection, so he did not take them.

We sat in a bathtub of cold water across from each other, knees huddled against our chests, silent. The halfmoons under his eyes were tinged purple, his skin pale but hot. He slept rarely; unconscious, he often spoke as though awake. Snores rattled his bony chest. He was crazier than me, his sadness deeper and longer.

I am my mother: impassive, reluctant to address my life as a thing that has happened to me. A man strangled me nearly to death my junior year of college. I spent the next year's winter remembering. The basement apartment became a tomb. I answered my mother's calls, left the apartment for classes. The astrophysicistpoet was quiet, his thin frame almost feminine. He satisfied, but did not threaten my body.

■■■

I could not shave my legs or look at my face in the mirror without thinking it frivolous, stupid even, to be human, when faroff stars burn and die, unnamed. Science tells us meaning does not exist outside the human brain—a terrible knowledge. Psychiatric drugs can alter the chemistry of the brain but cannot create a meaning that is not there. I took comfort in the concrete and the terrestrial: cold bathwater; orgasm; menstrual cramps; bony processes of knuckle, elbow, and knee.

I drank, and I drank, and I watched science documentaries. The idea of Pluto began to obsess me. A perfect, intact world—untainted by life, free of selfawareness.

The thought of suicide ran parallel to all others. Death seemed clean, seemed pure and Plutonian, safe. I no longer believed in the soul's journey through space and knew in death I would not be met by my disappointed grandmother, my pedophile grandfather, my tabby cat. I wrote through the winter, took antidepressants, and the spring thaw found me alive beneath thick ice.

■■■

My first year of graduate school, *D'Aulaire's Book of Greek Myths* sits on my bookshelf between a cozy mystery lent to me by my mother and Defoe's *Moll Flanders*.

Drawn in the same muted pencil, Hades and his captured queen Persephone stand under a ceiling of stalactites and glinting jewels, draped in funereal robes, the whites of their eyes prominent against ashen skin. Hades holds a forked staff; his face seems pained. Persephone endures—quiet, stoic. Unnoticed at first, the souls of the dead surround the unhappy couple—a hundred or more tiny specters, nearly invisible.

The book says, *Sooner or later, all mortals came to Hades. Once inside his realm, they whirled about forever like dry leaves in a cold autumn wind.*

■ ■ ■

Pluto follows the cerulean gas giant Neptune as an afterthought, both beyond and beneath us in directionless space. Mute rock, quiescent under layers of nitrogen ice. Poised at the periphery of our Sun's grip.

I imagine Pluto as both god and geography. A vessel holding the swell of what I cannot know. I think of my father, dark and belowground; my mother, bright but distant.

NASA's New Horizons spacecraft will approach Pluto in 2015, with plans of flyby study. We will for the first time be privy to that guarded world, its dark contours illuminated. ■

LAUNDRY WOMAN

My great-grandmother agitated
Mrs. Worldly's wash every week
over the hot flash and glow
of the fire in the misery shed.
Hand on rough stick, grandmother
pulled around the glob
of tangled shirts and sheets;
she stirred as if hauling the weighted
laundry about an axis, sloshy seas
yielding a watery soup, thin gruel, sure,
but nutrition enough to feed her
fatherless children, nutrition enough
to bring us into this unimagined World.

KATHLEEN DRISKELL

WHAT I LEARNED IN MY MOTHER'S KITCHEN

While my father traveled for his job during the week,
my mother lived the life of a woman emancipated
by TV dinners and pizza delivery. On Sundays, though,
after church, my father dragged her back to the kitchen,
where she worked the opener against the lip of a can
of salmon so awkwardly I stuck around to make sure
that when she fished out the snaggle-toothed lid,
she didn't cut herself and need some stitches. While her
cigarette smoldered in the pink melamine ashtray,
she sputtered, crushing the tiles of saltines with her
manicured hands, plunging ten fingers, tips painted bright
pink, into the bowl of heaped cracker dust and grey skin.
I watched her jaw tighten when through her powerful fists,
she squeezed and crunched the fragile feathery bone.

KATHLEEN DRISKELL

EVOLUTION

Aspiring to college,
I set out
to evolve more quickly
than the finches
and tortoises
I'd read about, and more
quickly than the coal-miners
and factory workers
I'd come from and
after just one summer
in loose brown polyester,
and awful white shoes,
the required waitress uniform
at the Country Club,
where I set limp Dover Sole
in front of lunching ladies
I moved into the hot tuxedo
I wore at a 5-star, where tableside
I often cracked a coddled egg
and divided the bulb of yolk yellow
from the sticky white viscosity
and addressed the anchovy,
until its hairy bones were mashed,
and then the lemon squeeze,
and the Tabasco, eight quick drops.
Sitting next to the older men
in expensive suits and shoes,
young beautiful women
in narrow sequined dresses
tried to ignore me as I tossed

their garlicky salad,
and deftly used my Russian
service. With each of them,
I was just as haughty, plating
their leafy vinegary greens
with disdain, because like Darwin,
I hadn't seen, at first, that these
women were determined to evolve, too.

KATHLEEN DRISKELL

Kathleen Driskell

AN *APPALACHIAN HERITAGE*
INTERVIEW WITH

KATHLEEN DRISKELL

"I've had a lot of different experiences with graveyards," says Kathleen Driskell. As a child growing up in rural Peewee Valley outside of Louisville, she often hopped a fence to visit an old Confederate cemetery near her home. "My mother and father argued all the time, and to get away from them I would go over there, and I remember reading—riding my bike over there and reading."

Back then, the young Driskell had no idea that she would grow up to become a national bestselling poet, the author of acclaimed poetry collections including *Seed Across Snow*. Nor could she have known that her childhood graveyard experience would help prepare her for another one, just outside her kitchen window, that would turn her to the page to contemplate loss and mortality—and what we leave behind. These themes are woven throughout her latest collection, *Next Door to the Dead*, published in late 2015 by the University Press of Kentucky. Inspired by her years living in an old country church adjacent to a crumbling graveyard, Driskell considers the lives of the dead and their families, creating a book that is steeped in mystery and deep beauty.

She recently spoke to *Appalachian Heritage* about crafting the book, a forthcoming poetry collection centered on manners and blue-collar service, and her life in the classroom at Spalding University.

JASON HOWARD: You and your husband live in a pre-Civil War era country church that you all converted into a house and has figured into your writing. What attracted you all to this house?

KATHLEEN DRISKELL: It was a Lutheran church... there was some kind of schism. And so somebody got mad and said, "We're not going to that [church]," and I think it was a little too progressive for them. This was the more conservative church...And then it changed hands. There were a lot of rumors about what it was. We've had some of the old neighbors who said, "Yeah, I remember when the snake handlers were there, and the Pentecostals were there." But they would talk about how they would put their speakers out in the trees, and have services so that everyone could hear for miles around. And then we bought it from a conservative Christian—they were called Public Baptist. We saw a for sale sign on it. We were looking for another property. And we were like reading the map or whatever and Terry said, "Let's look and this!" And I'm like, "Oh god, no! What are you talking about?" So he'd crawled under the house before I could stop him. And he came back out and said, "We're buying it!"

When we moved in, it had been empty for about three or four years I think. [It was] just old and creaky and dark in here. There were condoms and beer cans and cigarette wrappers all over the place. So [teenagers] had been partying here. And then there was a room where there was a pentagram by the pulpit. It was not a really feel-good place.

JH: There's a graveyard next door, but when you all bought the place, someone—the preacher, the realtor, whoever—said that it was no longer in use.

KD: The preacher told me. I asked him flat out, and he said that it was full up and it's been full up. You know, I think that I just asked because I was curious. I don't know that [it] would have made any difference to me. I just don't think about graveyards that way. Since I've written this book and people have been talking to me about it, I never really have thought about them as being spooky places.

And the graveyard was really grown over for years and years and years. When we first moved in a lot of the headstones, the really ancient ones, were knocked over, and we would see kids over there all the time. We were just tormented by teenagers for the first ten years. [They would go there and] smoke, drink, get drunk, knock things over. And then when we moved in we sort of became the enemy because we'd say, "Hey! Get out of there! What are you kids doing?" We were like the old men on the lawn…even though that's not the way we thought about ourselves.

JH: How did you find out that the graveyard was still in use?

KD: Well the first time—I wrote about this in a poem in *Next Door to the Dead*—we had just moved in, we'd only been here a couple months. I was coming home from the grocery store—I was trying to get ice cream in, you know. And Wyatt [Driskell's son] was little. When I came home everybody had blocked the [driveway] and there were cars all over the place. And there was a hearse. [laughs] And I was like, "Holy mother of god!" You know, I was trying to be pretty respectful but the dogs were barking cause I was home. People were moving back and forth in their dark coats. I guess maybe there have been maybe eight or nine burials there since we've moved in. But it's always surprising.

JH: Your new poetry collection was inspired by this graveyard. How did you start writing the book?

KD: The reason I started writing the book was because one of the graves out there was from a neighbor's son who was twenty-three. On his way home—just had a baby, [a] girlfriend, [was] getting married—some young woman had a flat tire. He helped her [and] got hit by a semi that was going by. [He was in a coma], and the way I found out that he'd died was because I looked up from the laundry room window and two gravediggers were coming, dragging shovels. They do it the old fashioned way over there. That's the first time I've seen gravediggers over there. It was just—I mean I don't want to make it sound too arty, but it was just this metaphor, you know, the gravediggers are coming. And I knew exactly what it meant. And then, not only that [but] it's just different when a young person dies. [The graves here] are mostly elderly people, and they were maybe the last of their families that were going to be buried here. And then you hardly see [their families] again. But just watching his service, and the young people just heaving and hanging on each other.

JH: It's a different kind of grief.

KD: It is. And they're young so they don't go away. They keep coming. So over the years there's been this sort of steady parade. And then there's a Wildcats flag [on the grave]. There's a little Christmas tree that lit up. There's always something different.

That's how [the book] got organized. I might have been writing poems about the graveyard...but that was really when I started to cohese around the idea [of] what it meant to have old graves and new graves, and graves of people who were elderly and people who were very young.

JH: Did the poems start coming fast after you got the idea?

KD: I'm not a really fast writer, but this book came faster than any book that I've done. So once I start thinking about it, they came pretty quickly. It's interesting—it's almost like, you know when you're writing, you'll hear poets talk about how writing in the form of the sonnet really is freeing? Having that form frees you? It feels kind of like the half, the three-quarter acre of the graveyard was very freeing, because I soon found that I could write about whatever I wanted even though I was writing about a really small plot of ground there. So in *Next Door to the Dead* I have domestic violence poems, I have a lot of anti-war poems...a lot of relationship poems, poems about mothering, that sort of thing. I have poems that are pretty historical. It kind of freed me to do whatever I wanted to do.

JH: That makes me think of your poem "Tchaenhotep: Mummy at the Kentucky Science Center," which is in the book.

KD: Well, that poem I have been trying to write for about twenty-five years. Seriously. And it wasn't until I started writing this book that I was able to write it. I found a way into it.

JH: And you have Colonel Sanders and his wife, who obviously aren't buried here.

KD: No.

JH: But you were able to transcend [this particular] place—
KD: Yeah, that was a pretty pointed strategy in the book because I didn't want it to be macabre, really I wanted people to be surprised by it. So I started looking for epitaphs and things...and then I would take whatever the epitaph was and make a poem from it, like [my poem] "Dear Departed Dave." I wanted the book to lighten in certain places. I mean, obviously it's still about death and mortality and all that, but I still wanted to lighten it.

JH: How were you able to do that, to find humor in [what is] for most people a heavy, heavy subject?

KD: I think that people—we have jokes about death all the time, and we have tons of euphemisms that are kind of funny. I was going to go through this vein of euphemisms, you know like "pushing up daisies." But I also… wanted it to be about—Silas [House] said something one time I'll never forget. Someone was asking him about writing and death, and he said, "When we're writing about death we're really writing about love." And when he said that I thought that is so true. And so I don't think it's a book about death. I think it's a book about love, or trying to find love. I mean, I just have a different view—maybe because I've thought about this all the time because I look out the window and see it all the time. It weights me, but it's not like a burden, it's more like a ballast, if that makes sense. If you sit there and you look and you watch people come in and out of the graveyard, you think about your own kids, and your family members, and the people you love, and how you want to treat them that day…

The way that I think about Judeo-Christian ideals and tenets is…in metaphor. I think about the young woman bringing her daughter to visit [her father's] grave out there. And I think that's like heaven. You know, heaven's not in a cloud with somebody [holding] a little notepad saying you get in or you get out. Heaven is what you leave in the mind of others. And also you know, you think about, like, hell. You can leave hell in the mind of others, too. I'm looking out [at the graveyard], and I want to be as good as I can, leave good memories for my children, try to be heroic if I can in my little ways, try to treat other people kindly, so that there's a little piece of heaven left in their minds about me. And that's why writing is so important, too. Really we're talking about leaving stories.

JH: I love that you include animals in the book, and one image and metaphor that you keep coming back to is birds. Do they have a particular resonance with you?

KD: I'm really aware [of] birds there—I don't know if it's because in the wintertime you can see them in the trees or whatever. We see a lot of hawks out here, we see a lot of vultures, buzzards out here. I'm interested in birds. I really didn't realize that there were that many birds in the book until [a] reader pointed it out to me. It kind of makes sense to me...you've got birds lifting, taking flight. I remember reading [about] burial rites in Tibetan culture, where they take you to the top of the mountain and leave you there and the buzzards eat you and raise you up to heaven.

JH: That's a great image.

KD: Isn't it? I know. You get lifted up. And there's some of that in that poem "Praise"...with the deer at the side of the road being lifted up in that way. That was kind of on my mind, too. I mean I knew there were birds, but I didn't know there were zillions and zillions of birds in there.

JH: You have another poetry collection, *Blue Etiquette*, which will be published by Red Hen Press this fall. What's that book about?

KD: I seem to have obsessions about things, [which] helps me organize and start a project, and I can move out from there. I found a copy...in an old bookstore of Emily Post's *Book of Etiquette*, and sometimes it's called the *Blue Book of Etiquette* because it [had] a blue linen cover when it was first published. I just became fascinated...by the funeral rites in it and how to hold a home funeral. But then I started moving into the servants...and I realized that my folks would have been the servants she was talking about managing...So I've written some poems that kind of riff off that. I've written poems about silverware, like an oyster fork, or a fruit knife. We didn't have such things in my house when I was growing up.

When I was working my way through school—I was first generation—I got a job at The Seelbach [Louisville's legendary hotel] when it reopened in 1982, and it had a four-star restaurant. The guy...who was our maître d [illegible] wanted to make sure that we were really schooled. He actually came from Provence where he'd been in the hotel business, and so he taught me a lot about wine, he taught me about the mother sauces. And not too long after that I was a captain there. So I do know a lot about manners, but I learned it from being trained to serve other people. And so that was kind of a fascinating idea. I have restaurant poems in there, I have working class poems, I have a poem about the summer before I went to school [when] I worked mowing fairways at a golf club in Oldham County.

Emily Post [was] a really great writer—she's really entertaining. I have poems that are kind of done in her [voice].

[She] created these archetypes like the worldlies, and the young marrieds, and the know-nothings, and she uses [and] moves them around in her book to say what you should and shouldn't do. You know, the guildings, the old lineages. And so I created...poems around those characters.

JH: Some of those poems are connected to your ancestors back in West Virginia. You were raised in Oldham County [outside of Louisville], but did you grow up hearing a lot of stories about the mountains?

KD: Even after my family moved down here, we would go back to my grandmother's house and they would just tell stories. That's what the women did in the family...And so the men would be watching football, and we'd [all] be eating pie, and I would be under the table listening to it. But I have this really amazing image—like when someone would come in from West Virginia—and someone would talk about something that happened, and inevitably someone would go get the box. It was a cardboard box, all ripped up, and it was full of photographs. And they would just sift through it—

JH: Probably at the dining table—

KD: —at the dining table. And they would bring out a photograph. I mean, it's no wonder I'm a poet and I think about images first, you know. And they would look at a photograph, and then the stories would come. And so at least once a year we would go back...and stay there, because my great-grandfather [lived on] Black Panther Mountain and had some land there. So, yeah, lots of stories came from there.

JH: You've taught for a number of years at Spalding University, where you serve as Professor of Creative Writing and Associate Program Director of the low-residency MFA in Writing program, which has been consistently ranked as one of the best in the country. What do you think sets Spalding's program apart from others, and why should writers consider applying and attending?

KD: Our teaching philosophy is to emotionally support our students, and that's something that's been established from the very beginning. My pedagogical core is the same—I've always believed that you need to be constructive and supportive. And that doesn't mean we don't tell each other the truth—it just means we take the time to figure out how the truth can be received. [Creative writing programs] can be kind of cruel places. Particularly in graduate school, there's a lot of competition for not too much attention, and so people feel better about their own work by knocking people down. And that's just not something that we or I have ever believed in, because I know that when someone is really cruel to you in a workshop, your ears shut down...and so the learning stops. It's not that we're just being nice to be nice, but it's because it's the best way to teach and the best way to receive.

We have a really wide, diverse faculty, [and] I think we're always trying to make the program exciting by doing new things. And I think this is true of a lot of low-res programs, but particular to us, there are a lot of older students there. It's getting younger, but our average student is about forty-two. So these are people who have wanted to do this thing all their lives. Most of us [running the program] are writers and have MFAs, too. So we know—I know what it means, I know what it costs, and I know what it means to take this time away from your life, your family, your retirement funds or whatever. It's not cheap. But it's so important. I just think we're makers. You know, I think writing is one of the ways that's really accessible to a lot of us, whether we end up being great novelists or not.

What I always [tell] prospective students is the only reason they [should] get an MFA with us is because [they] can't imagine not doing it. And that's the only kind of student I want there. Sometimes they slip by me, and they're doing it just to be credentialed to teach college, which is a huge mistake because the market is so tight. And I never lie to prospective students about that...That's not the reason to come. [It's about wanting] to study in a great community of writers.

JH: I've heard that you're working on a novel.

KD: I am. [It's about] a young, adolescent coming of age, living in a church, whose parents were nonbelievers, who had been transplanted from someplace else, and came into the Bible Belt. I want to write a book about tolerance—not only the tolerance of religious people towards nonbelievers, but tolerance of nonbelievers toward the religious, because I think that nonbelievers often are a bit arrogant about faith...

But within a span of about a year some really horrible things happened right within this mile here. My neighbor was coming across the street to get her mail and a car hit her and dragged her...She survived, but she has some brain damage. Two teenage boys...skipped school, grabbed a canoe, went in Floyd's Fork [which runs behind here] and they were both drowned. We saw helicopters going over one night and found out later that some John had picked up a prostitute, slit her throat, and dumped her on the highway back here. And she crawled up the hill, and crawled into [a] car, and they found her the next day and she lived! A house burned down. Just all kinds of crazy stuff.

JH: That's a lot.

KD: It is a lot. And so I started thinking, you know, maybe there's something to this. So it's kind of about…what haunts us, and what is truly haunting. ■

FISH

My first was a nightcat, mud-yellow, spined,
hauled from the basement of the river
in Steubenville. It stabbed my palm,
marked me with a warning
punctuation.

Then a bass, fingerling, from a strip-mine pond,
slender and bright as a case knife's blade,
its jutted lower jaw
ripped by the hook.

How it lingered a moment
when I tossed it back,
as if cursing me
as it caught its breath
and mine.

And the one in the mind, forever
unlanded, vivid and immortal
before the altar of my myth:
a lunker shovelhead, snagged
just above some old wicket dam upriver,
wild country on either shore,
no houses for miles,
me in a leaking boat near dawn,
fog closing in—
and the sweet singing of the reel
as it runs my line
quick in that dying night.

RICHARD HAGUE

BLESS ITS HEART:
THE IRONY OF APPALACHIAN LITERATURE

MAURICE MANNING

A Ramble to Yonder England in which the Author Discovers the Romantic Roots of Appalachian Literature

In June 2009 I was doing field research in England around Nether Stowey, the village in the county of Somerset where Samuel Taylor Coleridge and his young family were living in 1797. It was in this place that Coleridge first met William Wordsworth and his sister, Dorothy. I was armed with a topographic map and a sheaf of antique poems. My goal was to take the very same poetry-inspiring walks Coleridge and the Wordsworths took more than 200 years ago. I realized what they were trying to do: to write poems whose rhythms and process of thought matched the up-and-down geography of the setting. They wanted the physical, exterior world to initiate and influence whatever happened in the co-creating, interior world of the mind.

As I was walking in those English woods, it occurred to me that Wordsworth and Coleridge were basically hillbillies, despite their fancy education. The poems Wordsworth and Coleridge were writing in 1797 and 1798 came together in their still pioneering book, *Lyrical Ballads*. They were trying to do something new, but they were also returning poetry to something old, to the subjects of folklore and ballads, and, as they liked to claim, to the language of the common, rural person. Coleridge's best-known poem, "The Rime of the Ancient Mariner," is about a guy who can't quit telling a tale. His audience is a man on his way to a country wedding. One of Wordsworth's poems, "Resolution and Independence," features an old man who tramps through the countryside and wades into ponds and bogs to collect leeches, by letting them attach to his bare legs, so he can then sell the leeches to locals for folk remedies. These two English poets wanted to take the lives, the locations, and the language of humble, isolated people and transform those materials into serious literary art. That very same task has been shared by our forebears and many of us writing today to make a mark for what we now call Appalachian Literature. The effort we share with our Romantic cousins has been to transform what was originally an oral culture and set it on the page as a viable literary world, and to imagine the lives of humble, unlettered people with value and dignity.

Wordsworth and Coleridge were also aware of a feature of their historical moment in England that eerily prefigures what has been a constant feature of Appalachian culture—many of the local characters Wordsworth and Coleridge were bringing to life in poetry, were in fact dislocated people, uprooted families, solitary wanderers, roaming the countryside. Historically, there is a simple explanation for this: many rural people in eighteenth century England and Scotland were forced to leave the land they had farmed and maintained for generations as a result of the British legal policies known as the "clearances"; due to the ugly birth of the Industrial Revolution in England, many rural people were given the choice either to work in the nightmare of a factory or to emigrate to what were then the colonies.

On my mother's side of the family, I know this is exactly what happened. An ancestor who was kicked out of Scotland in the 1760s managed to get to western North Carolina, which looked a bit like home, moved up to southwestern Virginia, which also looked like home, and eventually came through Cumberland Gap into southeastern Kentucky, which also looked like home, and thanks to the Revolutionary War, was now a viable American home, and so they stayed. While it's not accurate for all aspects of Appalachian culture, I think it can be claimed that parts of what we now call Appalachia were settled by exiles, and that what we now know as Appalachian Culture has been an unintentional by-product of the English Industrial Revolution. That suggests to me that Appalachian Literature has much in common with what we call African-American Literature, or any literature created by immigrants, refugees, or the disenfranchised. Yet almost as soon as the exiles from England and Scotland settled a place they could finally be, forces often from outside the region, but also within it, began to malign and destroy the place itself. Clear cutting, coal mining, mountaintop removal, and now fracking, have from the beginning made parts of the land upon which Appalachian culture took root unlivable. The destruction of the very land upon which the culture is planted is one of the defining features of Appalachia; it is a factor that goes beyond irony and has become a paradox. As much as we are rooted people, we have also been again and again uprooted, taking our culture with us wherever we roam.

Unlike the American frontier, which was settled by wave after wave of new people, Appalachia was settled by old people, or better said, by people whose ways were already old.

Even though we can align the first written literature from our region with the historical literary period known as Modernism, I think Appalachian Literature is much more Romantic in origin. The literature may be Modern in the academic sense, but the culture is not. When the first works of Appalachian Literature began to appear, largely through songs and ballads collected by folklorists, the region was still young—settled for maybe 100 years or so—but the settlers brought with them from England and Scotland and Ireland the traditions and bonds of a much older world. Unlike the American frontier, which was settled by wave after wave of new people, Appalachia was settled by old people, or better said, by people whose ways were already old. Or, a simpler way to express this foundational irony of Appalachian Literature, is to say Appalachian Literature is a twentieth century form of cultural expression, yet the culture itself goes back to the late eighteenth century, when it was already an old culture, uprooted and on the move to a new place.

I'm a Banjo-Playing Girl

My trip to England several years ago yielded this kind of literary-kinship discovery. At the end of my visit I was in London for a few days and attended a service in Westminster Abbey. It was a Sunday afternoon and the service was mostly music. On the way out we walked under the gigantic, thunderous pipes of the organ, which were elevated about twenty feet off the floor. For the time it took me to walk under the pipes, I realized I was part of the instrument, I was inside those vibrating columns of air, and my whole body was vibrating in the unity of sound.

For a few years I thought of this moment underneath the towering, cascading organ as a singular experience, something bound to that place and time. But I was wrong. More recently, I was taking banjo lessons near my home in Kentucky from my teacher, Sue Massek, a member of the pioneering Reel World String Band. She was teaching me some songs by Lily Mae Ledford, the leader of the Coon Creek Girls, who began playing at the famed Renfro Valley Barn Dance in the 1930s. Sue told me that Lily Mae's mother had not wanted her to learn an instrument and play music because it would lead her down the road of sin. But Lily Mae was determined, and she taught herself to play and sing by climbing up the hillsides in Powell County, Kentucky, to the rock houses, the natural amphitheaters left in the eroded cliffs. The acoustics of such a natural place are remarkable, and singing in such a place must be similar to my experience of walking under the organ pipes at Westminster Abbey—the physical place itself becomes part of the instrument. And here is one conclusion I draw from that coincidence: Appalachian Literature begins with sound, with the visceral experience of a voice in the moment of speaking or singing, or the crack or clop or clinking of some work, some task involving the hands and the body in a place that cradles and echoes the sound. Some literature begins in the mind, with a thought quivering in the rational mind, but I think Appalachian Literature begins with the embodied sound, with the voice, and the character suggested by the voice, and the attention that voice pays to the sound of the world around it.

Two Riddles From My Father and a Rusty from Pappy Taylor

My father tells the story of a summer night in the late 1930s when his father, a cousin, some fellows, and the undertaker were playing poker in Manchester, Kentucky. They were gathered at the home of the undertaker and were outside because of the heat. They were using a coffin the undertaker had recently made as a table. Apparently it didn't occur to any of the characters involved that there was anything unusual or morbid or weirdly symbolic about playing cards on the top of a coffin. If this were *Pilgrim's Progress* or Chaucer or Edmund Spenser, this situation would be allegorical, but in an Appalachian context, it's perfectly normal. There was plenty of moonshine going around, too. Eventually, the cousin, a tiny man named Jimmy "Parrot" White, had too much to drink and passed out. That prompted the other men to lay Cousin Jimmy in the coffin and carry it to the courthouse lawn. As the sun rose the next morning, the other men were gathered in the shade watching. Once the sun was up and the coffin got hot Jimmy Parrot woke, kicked off the coffin top, sat up, looked around and shouted, "Hellfire, boys, it's Judgment Day and I'm the first son-of-a-bitch here!"

The story has stayed with me for many years. It strikes me as a perfectly Appalachian story, a potent mix of dread and humor. It's doubtful that "Parrot" was educated; he may not have been terribly literate, but to my ear and mind he's a certified literary character.

Some years later when my Dad was just returned from the Korean War, Jimmy "Parrot" White was central to yet another story. He learned Dad was home and sent word to Dad and his brother, Ikey, that his roof was leaking and in need of repair. When they got there they looked around. It was raining, but Jimmy's roof seemed sound. Dad said, "Jimmy, I don't think you have a leak, the roof looks fine to me." Jimmy was in his bed—likely from being drunk. He reached under the bed, pulled out a pistol and fired it twice into the ceiling. "By God, it'll leak now!" he said.

When I was a boy we had a neighbor named Pappy Taylor. He was a great banjo player and had played on radio programs in the 1920s and 1930s. On the Fourth of July, 1975, several neighbors got together for a cookout and Mr. Taylor's bluegrass band played that evening. Between songs, Mr. Taylor would tell where he'd first learned a song, or he'd tell a joke. One of his jokes went like this:

> *Did I ever tell you 'bout my bald-headed uncle? Feller sold shoes. One day this big ole woman come in the store and was a tryin' on shoes. Well, my uncle was down there tryin' to get her big foot in the shoe. She looked down, saw his bald head and thought it was her bare knee. She tuck the hem of her dress and throwed it over his head, liked to smother him to death right thar!*

Each of these anecdotes is "Appalachian," because of the location where they occurred, and because the vernacular is distinct to our region. But I think each of these little tales is also literary. First of all, the language is more than mere vernacular; the thought expressed by each instance of vernacular is literary, because the language reveals the mind of the character, how that mind thinks, beyond the visceral sound of the utterance. These are also dramatic situations: there are characters brought together around a specific event, and each, in a classical sense, has a conflict. Best of all, though, each conflict is resolved with a twist. The poker players all thought they were going to pull a fast one on Jimmy Parrot, but none of them could have anticipated Jimmy's epiphany that it was Judgment Day and he had rose from the dead. Nor, some years later, could my father and uncle have expected Jimmy Parrot to shoot a couple of holes in his roof. The character intended to be the butt of the joke, turns the dramatic situation suddenly and deftly around through quick wit and perfectly-timed language, and in both cases that final flourish introduces a completely different register of language to the literary circumstance.

I share these stories to suggest that a tale-telling culture such as Appalachia is innately literary, even if the tales do not appear in print...

Pappy Taylor's tall-tale also has a distinct literary quality, and includes some satisfyingly subtle details. The detail that stands out to me is the fact that the woman was wearing a dress. That cultural point is implicit—this was a time when women in the mountains only wore dresses. I also love the phrase, "liked to smother him to death." It's interesting as grammar. "Liked to" is used to mean "almost" or "nearly," which are adverbs. Ordinarily, an adverb augments the action of the sentence, but in this case the adverb diminishes the action, and yet by being diminished, the action—a woman pulling her dress over a man's head—is ironically exaggerated, the whole scene is more uncomfortable, by being harmless in the end. And then I have never gotten the phrase "smother him to death" out of my mind's ear. Grammatically, it's redundant, but the double emphasis in this case has a similar effect as the diminishing adverb: ordinarily redundancy is glaring, but in this case it exaggerates the action and transforms a joke that ends with the word, "death," into genuine humor.

I share these stories to suggest that a tale-telling culture such as Appalachia is innately literary, even if the tales do not appear in print, and even if the region itself has been characterized as being illiterate. And these tales are further literary because even though they are rooted in a local realm, they manage to "translate" to the larger realm of all human experience—redemption, violence, and humor are pretty well universal. Literary people are clever that way.

Other Voices, Or: Will the Real Hillbilly Please Stand Up

Consider the following variety of literary voices, beginning with Robert Hayden, a poet born in Detroit, but part of whose work was to imagine backward—that is, to imagine African-American experience in the South, before and along the way to the great migration North.

And when that ballad lady went
to ease the lover whose life she broke,
oh surely this is the road she took,
road all hackled through the barberry fire,
through cedar and alder and sumac and thorn.

Red clay stained her flounces
and stones cut her shoes
and the road twisted on to his loveless house
and his cornfield dying
in the scarecrow's arms.

And when she had left her lover lying
so stark and so stark, with the Star-of-Hope
drawn over his eyes, oh this is the road
that lady walked in the cawing light,
so dark and so dark in the briary light.[1]
—"A Road in Kentucky"

Now consider this stanza from Kentucky poet and writer Robert Penn Warren's later poem "What Voice at Moth-Hour":

What voice did I hear as I wandered alone
In a premature night of cedar, beech, oak,
Each foot set soft, then still as stone
Standing to wait while the first owl spoke?[2]

Last I heard, Warren was considered a Fugitive and an Agrarian, and even a New Critic; but he hasn't been thought of as a card-carrying Appalachian writer.

Now a verse paragraph from "Monadnoc" by Ralph Waldo Emerson:

Now in sordid weeds they sleep,
Their secret now in dullness keep;
Yet, will you learn our ancient speech,
These the masters who can teach.
Fourscore or a hundred words
All their vocal muse affords;
These they turn in other fashion
Than the writer or the parson.
I can spare the college-bell,
And the learned lecture, well;
Spare the clergy and libraries,
Institutes and dictionaries,

For the hardy English root
Thrives here, unvalued, underfoot.
Rude poets of the tavern hearth,
Squandering your unquoted mirth,
Which keeps the ground, and never soars,
While Jake retorts, and Reuben roars;
Tough and screaming, as birch-bark,
Goes like a bullet to its mark,
While the solid curse and jeer
Never balk the waiting ear.
To student ears the keen relished jokes
On truck, and stock, and farming-folks,—
Nought the mountain yields thereof
But savage health and sinews tough.[3]

Emerson is writing about hillbillies, albeit the hillbillies he encountered in New Hampshire way back in 1845. Isn't it refreshing to discover one of the founders of American Transcendentalism, a writer who is rightly identified as a philosopher, found something vital and fundamentally literary in the hillbilly world, and especially in the unlettered tongue?

Here's some more verse, this time by Stephen Vincent Benet from his epic poem about the Civil War, *John Brown's Body*:

Now listen to me, you Tennessee corn,
  And listen to my word,
This is the first child ever born
  That was christened by a bird.

1 Hayden, Robert. *Collected Poems.* (New York: Liveright, 2013), 31.
2 Warren, Robert Penn. *The Collected Poems of Robert Penn Warren.* John D. Burt, ed. (Baton Rouge: LSU Press, 1998), 475.
3 Emerson, Ralph Waldo. *Collected Poems and Translations.* Harold Bloom and Paul Kane, eds. (New York: The Library of America, 1994), 54.

He's going to act like a hound let loose
When he comes from the blackjack tree,
And he's going to walk in proud shoes
All over Tennessee.

I'll feed him milk out of my own breast
And call him Whistling Jack.
And his dad'll bring him a partridge nest,
As soon as his dad comes back.[4]

John Brown's Body is a masterpiece, now sadly neglected. But it won the Pulitzer Prize in 1929 and there are hillbillies all over it, although Benet wasn't one himself. Benet was a graduate of Yale and was a significant literary figure for his time. He resided in New York City, but also had a home in Augusta, Georgia. In those days he would have traveled by train through the mountains. I like to think he had his ears open during his travels.

Here are a few stanzas from a Gothic ballad-poem, "Old Christmas." Two women are meeting each other at dawn:

Where you coming from, Lomey Carter,
So airly over the snow?
And what's them pretties you got in your hand,
And where you aiming to go?

Step in, Honey: Old Christmas morning
I ain't got nothing much;
Maybe a bite of sweetness and corn bread,
A little ham meat and such,

But come in, Honey! Sally Anne Barton's
Hungering after your face.
Wait till I light my candle up:
Set down! There's your old place.[5]

The poem goes on to reveal a double-murder, and we learn that Lomey Carter is already a ghost. It's Old Christmas and ghosts can walk the earth until dawn, and elderberry bushes bloom, "and critters kneel down in their straw." This sounds pretty authentic. As I have said, some of the first Appalachian literature was recorded or taken down by writers who also had an interest in folklore. One of those poets, Roy Helton, began "tramping" through North Carolina, Tennessee, and Kentucky around 1915. He was drawn to the dialect, to the language, to the landscape, and to the ballad-tale. And he wrote "Old Christmas," among many other poems in the voices of Appalachian characters. This poem, in fact, was the first poem I heard that sounded like the voice of my grandmothers. I was a senior in high school; the poem has stayed with me ever since—in fact, it's sort of haunted me. Yet, Roy Helton was from Washington, D.C. and spent much of his adult life in Philadelphia. Should we consider "Old Christmas," a poem many of us recall from school, Appalachian literature?

Now let's consider some prose with two passages from the early chapters of *Moby Dick*, published in 1851:

> *... it's a nice bed: Sal and me slept in that ere bed the night we were spliced. There's plenty room for two to kick about in that bed; it's an almighty big bed that. Why, afore we give it up, Sal used to put our Sam and little Johnny in the foot of it. But I got to dreaming and sprawling about one night, and somehow, Sam got pitched on the floor, and came near breaking his arm.*

Arter that, Sal said it wouldn't do. Come along here, I'll give ye a glim in a jiffy;" and so saying he lighted a candle and held it towards me, offering to lead the way.[6]

And now this passage from a few pages earlier:

He stood full six feet in height, with noble shoulders, and a chest like a coffer-dam. I have seldom seen such brawn in a man. His face was deeply brown and burnt, making his teeth dazzling by the contrast; while in the deep shadows of his eyes floated some reminiscences that did not seem to give him much joy. His voice at once announced that he was a Southerner, and from his fine stature, I thought he must be one of those tall mountaineers from the Alleganian Ridge in Virginia.[7]

These two excerpts are set in the whaling port of New Bedford, Massachusetts, a location not usually found on the map of Appalachia.

And here is some more prose, from one of the most gorgeous literary essays I know—D.H. Lawrence's "Nottingham and the Mining Countryside"—that discovers the metaphysical in the physical:

When the men came up into the light, they blinked. They had, in a measure, to change their flow. Nevertheless, they brought with them above ground the curious dark intimacy of the mine, the naked sort of contact, and if I think of my childhood, it is always as if there was a lustrous sort of inner darkness, like the gloss of coal, in which we moved and had our real being.[8]

Lawrence is writing in the late 1920s looking back to the mid-nineteenth century in rural England, but couldn't this passage equally describe features of the Appalachian experience in the mid-twentieth century?

And still more prose, this from British short-fiction master and travel writer V.S. Pritchett:

> *The time was late September, the laurels were thick and dark in the woods. There was often rain. I climbed up forest paths to the "balds" at the top and down to the next creek. There were no inns. I simply knocked on the doors of the poor shacks and no one ever refused me; very rarely would they take money. Flies infested the food in the poorest places and you could see the stars through the gaps in the walls. The family might have a patch of maize on their steep farm. They passed the sugar cane through rollers and drained the molasses into a bucket and sometimes had a mule on a pole stirring something in a cauldron over a stick fire.*
>
> *The hillsides smelled of apples and chestnuts. The clothes of the women were cheap cotton made by themselves. I remember a wild-looking girl wearing only a sack with a hole in it stirring the apple butter in a cloud of flies. She smiled: there was often a soft, lostlooking smile on the women's bony faces.*[9]

4 Benet, Stephen Vincent. *John Brown's Body*. (New York: Rinehart & Co, 1928), 205-206.

5 Helton, Roy. *Lonesome Water*. (New York: Harper & Brothers, 1930), 27.

6 Melville, Herman. *Moby Dick*, (New York: Library of America, 1983), 813.

7 Ibid., 809.

8 Lawrence, D.H. *The Portable Lawrence*, edited by Diana Trilling. (New York: Viking Press, 1947), 617.

9 Pritchett, V.S. "Appalachian Spring" in *New York Review of Books*, Jan. 21, 1982.

In this essay—titled "Appalachian Spring" and published in the *New York Review of Books* in 1982—Pritchett is recalling the time in the 1920s he walked through the region of southern Appalachian that would become Great Smoky Mountain National Park. Some of the people he met on his first trip would soon be uprooted for the creation of the park. In 1982, Pritchett goes back and sees little sign of the world he first visited fifty-five years before.

"Appalachian Spring" is also the title of a musical composition by Aaron Copland—who was born in Brooklyn, New York. "Appalachian Spring" was first performed as an orchestral suite in 1944; the composition was awarded the Pulitzer Prize in 1945. Choreographer Martha Graham adapted the composition for ballet performance by the same title. It was the New York-based Graham who, surprisingly, suggested the title for Copland's composition, yet she got her idea from a section of Hart Crane's poem, "The Bridge." Here are the relevant lines from the Ohio-born Crane—who was writing from Brooklyn and France:

O Appalachian Spring! I gained the ledge;
Steep, inaccessible smile that eastward bends
And northward reaches in that violet wedge
Of Adirondacks! [10]

We have a ballet, a musical suite, two epic poems, a classic nineteenth century American novel about whaling life, an English Modernist's take on coal mining, a Transcendentalist's encounter with a mountain, a British writer's double-reflection on the Smoky Mountains, a folksy anthropological poem, and two more poems self-consciously working within the ballad form—and all of these varied artistic expressions have stuck themselves like beggar-lice onto the britches of Appalachia. My question is why? What is it about Appalachian culture that has prompted such a wide range of writers and artists to lay claim to it?

I Ain't Got No Teeth, I Done Married My Cousin, and I Can't Talk Right

I'm going to share something now that disturbed me greatly when I first read it. I was disturbed because it seemed driven by a sense of cultural superiority. But I was further disturbed by my own consideration that there may be a grain of truth in the assessment. I'm going to read now an excerpt from an article that surveys the state of poetry in the South. Following a summary and evaluation of poetry coming from more privileged sectors of the South, the authors are eager to extol the rich potential for what they call the literature of "the Negro." Their claim is because "Negro life" in the South is earthier, the literature that will eventually come from that culture will be genuine and authentic. Here is what these authors have to say as they conclude their discussion of "Negro" poetry and make the transition to their final claims.

> *The Negro, however, is not the only source of folklore in the South. Even richer in poetic material is the lofty back-country of the Appalachians. The rush of American civilization has thus far touched only the fringes of this rugged land ... The mountains of the Carolinas and Kentucky were settled in the days of Daniel Boone and earlier by sturdy Scotch-Irish and English pioneers who built their isolated settlements behind the ramparts of rock. There, sequestered from the flow and change of civilization, they have continued to live the life of the pioneer. There are certain districts in the Black and Great Smoky ranges where life has remained*

absolutely static for a century and a half. There it is still possible to hear old English ballads and folk-tales which passed from current use generations ago; and one still encounters Elizabethan words. Certainly nowhere else in the America of today can one find conditions so favorable to the development of genuine folk expression; with the background of an old, but still remembered civilization, and absolute isolation which encourages the crystallization, by word of mouth, of the idea into the story.

The mountaineer responds but little to beauty. In his great tumble of hills, which contains forty-six peaks of over six thousand feet, including the highest point east of the Rocky Mountains, amid a flora that is bewildering in its pageantry of color, he is stubborn, vindictive in anger, elemental as a child in his amusements, shrewd, silent, and unerring in his estimate of the 'furreners' he may chance to meet.

... In spite of the fact that the southern mountaineer is probably the most interesting and least known figure in our national life, it will be many years before he will write his own story, if ever. The lack of schools, and his rooted indifference to educational advantages, will keep him much as he is, but he should be transcribed through the medium of some art before he passes; for there is nothing else quite like him on the continent." [11]

10 Crane, Hart. *The Bridge: An Annotated Edition*. Lawrence Kramer, ed. (New York: Fordham University Press, 2011), 47.

11 Allen, Hervey & Dubose Hayward. "Poetry South" in *Poetry*, April 1922, 38-41.

That assessment and diagnosis comes from an article called "Poetry South," published in the April 1922 issue of *Poetry*, the same magazine that first published Ezra Pound, T.S. Eliot, H.D., and Wallace Stevens among others, and the same magazine that has provided the definitive record of American poetry for over a hundred years. The article was co-written by Hervey Allen and Dubose Hayward, literary friends from Charleston, South Carolina. Hayward also wrote the novel from which the New York-based Gershwin Brothers created the great American opera, *Porgy and Bess*. In other words, the excerpt I just read was intended to be authoritative; the writers were presenting themselves as credible experts on all of the poetry coming from the vast and diverse region of America known as the South, and they included the nascent literature of Appalachia in their number. I've read somewhere that Appalachia is the South of the South—a region of our country that is even marginalized by a larger marginalized region. As Kurt Vonnegut would say, so it goes.

This is the final, twinkling irony of Appalachian Literature: we have a viable literature in spite of the limits of our region, and despite the doubts and judgments of the literary establishment.

This is the final, twinkling irony of Appalachian Literature: we have a viable literature in spite of the limits of our region, and despite the doubts and judgments of the literary establishment. All we have to do is go forth and trust that the human imagination, wherever it resides, will call to life the things that matter to us all and present them as a pretty, a toy for thought and a wonder for the soul.

My Appalachia

Last spring I wrote a poem as I was trying to re-build our old tobacco barn. I found myself standing beneath the geometry of timbers, amazed by the still living structure and design—it struck me as an art. And then I noticed something small, that reached me as something human and therefore ambiguously vital.

An Iron Ring Fastened to a Rail in the Barn

I've got a banjo six feet long
and a red-handled Barlow knife,
so I've got the credentials, Mister, to do
the things I do. It takes a lot
of figuring and time to do it.
The barn is just an empty church,
a solemn spirit is inside it.
Something was tied to a rail—because
an iron ring is fastened there—
maybe to suffer, I don't know.
A world of art is in front of you,
not always elegant art, but art
that reveals its passion. I've decided
to love the elegant less than I love
the wild, the untamed passionate art.
The blurt and cackle of birds, the look
of a curled-up lower leaf on a tree,
the tree itself from underneath—
the unexpected shadowy shape.
This distance across the hills is something
you can hear, like a voice. It's space and time
and the sky-domed air and objects and trees,
the shapes of living things, the wonder

of everything, the only art.
Even a world that's surreal begins
with the world as it is in plain sight
and mystical for being itself.
And what am I to do, to add
to it my little portion of being?
Whoever heard of a six-foot banjo?
That's like playing a man—but playing a man
or a longish woman is something you have
to do if you're serious about
this art, and I don't mean poetry,
I mean the larger art of being
alive in the world and suddenly seeing
an iron ring and wondering what
was its use and if it was an art
and if there was suffering involved.
I've come to believe that art can be
a beautiful, necessary wound,
a piercing of the soul and then,
after a dark time, a joy.

I don't know if the puzzle pieces I have defined can be combined, and I don't know if they should. My inclination is to get more Hillbilly as I go, to challenge the status quo, to push back against the establishment, as any artist must, and see what happens. We are still going on, we are still making the literature of our region, and because Appalachian Literature is still in the process of being formed, it is still alive. ■

CROW

staggers with one fist foot
at the far end of the tanned pasture
among tufted horse cookies
fifty yards from the dozen critical others
whacking at frosted apples

It doesn't seem to miss the "murder"
as its called but maybe remembers
being and wanting to be among them
in woods and fields blown quiet
as winter wind sifting over aging snow
where they always made such noise together

a story an elder can make of the scene
this gimp feeding on dumped seeds
maybe anxious though that may not be
not by a long shot and not this day
just because it hops off kilter and pecks
and watches with cool discipline
one day at a time the foolishness

Unless the boy comes quietly down the road
with his new .22 Cal. Winchester plinker
desperate for something to kill
his fear like blued hope he must be rid of
called pity for the loner's solitude

a boy who will aim carefully
shoot like a man flushing any notions of boy
of crows from the field

that settles back into silence
the “Crack!” dying in trees

then lifts and inspects the brown-eyed
bundle he suddenly did not intend to kill

PAUL NELSON

WINTER'S RAVEN

black pickaxe in the winter blasted orchard
shattering a ceramic apple in spiculed grass
hops off kilter on one foot

having stood too long on sun wet
wind set lake-ice hacking at a junk fish
called roach and tossed by a local fisherman

its other foot obsidian in crystal
snapped off clambering into air
the unbridled yellow lab skidding toward it

leaving this perfect scrap this amulet
like the fly in amber to chisel out
that I noticed while skating

my honed edges etching figures in the surface
inexactly perfect as Picasso pencil curves
the bird no longer passerine

a gimp that hops and chops bits of fruit
that flip get lit by sunset glitz
shiny as his clucking family murder

satin robed and solemnly perched
judges on high benches
sitting tight above the neighborhood

PAUL NELSON

A QUEEN
IN MY BLUE JEANS

TESSA McCOY

1.

It is a week until Christmas and Momma is nodding out by the tree. In a thin cotton shift, she sits Indian style, one leg folded under the other, next to a kerosene heater trying to wrap presents. A burning cigarette in one hand. A pair of scissors in the other. A heap of ashes cradled in the fold of the gown between her knees.

Every time her chin hits her chest, she opens her eyes slightly as if she is straining against the weight of her own existence and says, "Get." When Momma's doing pills, she likes to be by herself. There's something lonely about the sound of a pill being crushed against a plate that reminds her of her past, of her failures, of her victories. Or so she says.

On nights like tonight, when Momma is real bad off, I stay near enough. I am afraid a lit cigarette will drop and burn the house down, and us with it, if she is alone. I am afraid she will stop breathing and no one will know and she will die. On nights when we pile up together and sleep in the same bed, I lie next to her with my hand on her belly. The uneven rise and fall of her breathing is never enough to put me to sleep, but it is enough to know that that night isn't the night.

"O Come All Ye Faithful" is playing in the background of a local car dealership commercial on TV. "Jesus saves and so do we! Money that is! Come all ye faithful to Carl Gregory of Johnson City—Johnson City, Tennessee!" Momma hates this commercial. She says it is cheap. I turn the volume up.

Momma stirs. She certainly looks faithful passed out against the Christmas tree like that. In this light, if I squint hard enough, she even looks like Mary, the Virgin Mother who, despite just giving birth to the Christ child, Savior of the world, still isn't ready for the commitment of a five year lease on a new or preowned Chrysler, Jeep, or Dodge.

2.

The baby's bottle spins around and around on a crusty glass plate. The piss-yellow light and hum of the microwave invite me to lie down on the cold linoleum and sleep. It is 1:30 am and in six hours the school bus will run. It is going to be a tough morning at school if I don't get some sleep, but the baby is crying. He is hungry.

In first grade, I was in a gifted program where I taught my classmates, who were struggling, how to read. At age four, spelling words like mountain posed no trouble at all because Momma taught me how to read and write before I started Kindergarten. "By God," she'd say, her dark hand covering mine, tracing letters in big blocky print, MOUNTAIN. MOUNTAIN. MOUNTAIN. MOUNTAIN. MOUNTAIN. MOUNTAIN, "I'll see to it that you do better than me."

Now, I am a freshman at Ervinton High School and my grades are slipping. It is too hard to think about classes, or grades, or anything much other than the baby and wonder if Momma is taking care of him when I'm not around.

One day last month, he pulled a hot iron down on his hand. Ruth, Momma's friend, took him to the hospital in Abingdon. When I came home from school, Momma was passed out on the couch and the baby was sitting in the middle of the floor sucking air through an empty baby bottle. His chubby hand was wrapped in light blue gauze with goldfish on it.

"The hospital said the baby has second-degree burns. I am sorry for leaving the iron plugged in," reads a note from Ruth that was laying on the floor next to Momma and a half empty case of beer. It went on to say she was going home to Grundy to take care of her Momma who was ill.

I didn't know if it was the accident with the hot iron that ultimately convinced Ruth to leave, or if it was the prospect of telling Momma face-to-face that she was to blame. What I did know for sure was that Momma spent the last of the money on beer, and that the baby was out of formula.

3.

"Don't tell Mammaw," Momma says as she licks the end of the joint, twists it, and hands it to me.

It's Tuesday, the night before Christmas, and "Yellow Submarine" is playing on 101.5 FM. I strike a match against the rough edge of the matchbook and put the flame to the twisted end of the joint. I inhale deeply and cough like someone just rammed a toilet bowl brush down my throat.

"Turn that damned thing up, John!" Aretha, Momma's good time friend and once was girlfriend, yells from the kitchen at her husband, but the way she says it sounds more like, "Jawwwn." He broke her nose in a fistfight sometime during the late 80s, Momma said, on account he thought she shorted him on some cocaine they bought together. Now her nose sits sigogglin, almost touching the side of her cheek, and her voice, once deep and thick with undertones of her native homeland, is nasally and piercing.

I don't know if he is ever going to stop shouting, or if he is ever going to let go and quit swaying us back and forth...

Momma is laughing and laughing, and the harder I cough the louder she laughs. Bosco, her current boyfriend, too new to know what he is really getting with Momma, wraps his hairy caveman arm around me and sways us back and forth to the music while shouting, "WE ALL LIVE IN A YELLOW SUBMARINE! YELLOW SUBMARINE! YELLOW SUBMARINE!"

I don't know if he is ever going to stop shouting, or if he is ever going to let go and quit swaying us back and forth, or if he will ever figure out that Momma will love him only as long as she is willing, and as long as she is willing depends on how many pills he has, or if Momma is ever going to stop laughing and wipe that red lipstick off her teeth, or if the radio will ever be loud enough for that woman with the nasally voice, or if the Beatles will ever sing something that will make me feel better about the future, or if someone will ever open the window so I can get some air because I am hot and suffocating, but by the time the joint gets back around to me "Hey Jude" is on the radio, I feel calm again, and Momma has quit laughing. She and Bosco have gone to the back of the trailer, to her and daddy's bedroom, and closed the door.

4.

When I hear his socked feet shuffling across the carpet, I know it's over.

"You're a real stallion, Bosco," Momma yells from the bedroom, but Bosco doesn't know what irony is. He blushes and reaches for his coat hanging near the door.

"See ya, kid," he says. His voice sounds like gravel under a pair of heavy boots. I like it. I like Bosco, even though his devotion to Momma reminds me of a baby bird, helpless and unable to fly. He doesn't know that Momma will push him out of the nest one day, regardless if he knows how to fly or not.

Last week, he gave me a twenty-dollar bill before he left and said, "Don't tell your Momma," and I didn't. When daddy died, she got $100,000 in life insurance money. She spent it on drugs, trips to the beach, and hair relaxer.

To be fair, she did buy my brothers and me some clothes and shoes. She also put us a CD in the bank with $10,000 a piece, accessible by her, and us only when we turned eighteen. Two months later, she withdrew the CDs and went to Sturgis.

The money is gone now. There's no trace of it either except for a faded tattoo on Momma's ankle of a pink dolphin, the color of wet seashells, jumping over shaky cursive that says, *Myrtle Beach 2002*. Just in case she ever forgets.

5.

"Come in here," Momma says. She wants to comb my hair like she used to when I was little. She likes to pretend she's the Momma she used to be when she drinks too much.

When I was young she combed my hair every night. She'd run her fingers through it and smooth it down until it shined. I felt loved with each tender tug of the brush, with each strand she affectionately untangled. In the wintertime, she would get up before dawn and build a fire in the old wood-burning stove and lay my clothes out next to it so they would be warm. We'd sit together under the covers and watch *Dumbo* until the school bus ran. She'd fast forward the part when Dumbo visited his Momma, who had been captured, because I would sob every time she reached her long trunk through the bars of the window to caress Dumbo while he cried for her. But now, I don't even hug Momma anymore and she has stopped trying.

"No, you can't comb my hair," I say. I can see it on her face that it hurts her.

"We grew up together, you know? I was seventeen when you was born. We grew up together." Momma is wrapped up in daddy's old grey t-shirt that says *Fournier*. He was a supervisor there when they were first married. He worked middle shift and me and Momma would go pick him up in the dead of night when it was time for him to come home because we only had one car. He would kiss Momma, every time, like he hadn't seen her in a century. Then he'd hand his red and white lunchbox to the backseat where green apple Warheads and a grape Hi-C waited for me at the bottom.

Now, the bedsheets are on the floor. The pink satin ones I was never allowed to put my feet on when I was little, and Momma is laying on the bed looking like maybe she misses green apple Warheads and grape Hi-C's, too.

"No, we didn't, Momma." She wants to believe it. She wants me to believe it and to tell her that I believe it, because if I do, it means I understand why she acts the way she does.

"We didn't grow up together at all," I say and close the bedroom door.

6.

It's Christmas Day and Mammaw is on the other end of the phone, "Come on down when y'all get ready, honey, and bring the baby's formula."

"I will, Mammaw," I say, throwing shoes and books at the bathroom door, trying to hurry Momma up. She's been in there for over an hour and the whole family is waiting on us to eat dinner.

But I hear the usual *crunch, crunch, crunch* of a pill being ground onto the sink followed by a long sniff, so I know she'll come sashaying out the bathroom like she's the queen of the trailer park any minute now.

But I hear the usual crunch, crunch, crunch *of a pill being ground onto the sink followed by a long sniff...*

Her sweater is too tight and she is wearing my blue jeans, but, when she opens the door, she looks real pretty.

Before she and daddy separated, there weren't many who could stand next to Momma and be noticed. Used to, women admired her confidence and called her high-spirited. Now they say she is just pathetic white trash who tries too hard. But Momma still walks around like she's a queen. A queen in my blue jeans. And I have no idea what that makes me.

"You ready?" she wipes at her nose and sniffs.

"Sure," I say.

"Before we go I want to give you this."

It's her wedding band, the only thing left of her marriage to daddy.

"Merry Christmas," she says and smiles.

"Momma," I say.

"Hmm?"

"You still got lipstick on your teeth."

I wasn't going to tell her, but I figured one good turn deserves another.

7.

We walk close together, arm-in-arm, our heads ducked against the cold. I haven't been this near to Momma in a long time. I've forgotten how her hair smells like cloves and freshly turned earth. I'd rather reach down and eat a lump of dirty snow than to tell her how nice it is to be near her again. Instead, I think about Bosco and what he said last night and how I believe him to be right. We all do live in a yellow submarine, and it's sinking. ■

WHEN THOSE DAYS COME

She had a retreat in the house
by the pond. It was her life,
and then she had gone
outside, just to watch
the frogs, to sit under
the pine tree. She tapped
the palmettos on her way,
point to point, and nodded
like a girl undressing
for a bath. Each day she convinced

herself it was her life because one day
she would become an old woman,
the one whose wrists will have to be held,
the one wanting soup. Her blessed room
was unread, a clearing
of darkness, a bottom lip torn
and ragged, filled with salt
and memories of grilled vegetables.

When those days come, the yard—
that had sworn years before to be her trumpet,
to be her church—will die.
The house will cling
to the suspended pines. Dirt will be
a mirror that shows a hand
no longer reaching into it.

TERRY ANN THAXTON

NATIVITY SCENE ON THE COURTHOUSE LAWN

So long since
I have heard
said the word
oxen;
what mechanics the word insists
upon stable faces—
what jaw, flexing caverns fleeting,
what imperial posture the industrious tongue
plotting the palate's ancient pasture,
steering and stopping a simple
breath into the landscape that is
oxen:
once the name given
for a gathering of a kind
of grazing mammal.
Was it King James amplified
on some Christmas Eve
by a minister, his annual delivery
on that load-bearing night, his
stacking dusty stock
on wintry palates for shipment?
  for there was no room for them
  in storage
The city turns them on at night
only, those thin acrylic bodies,
each in its breast a light bulb, their private shine
together a rotating agriculture
of the public sphere. I say the word
oxen and hear

it said. Joseph bows
in time, automatically, the baby
kicks and reaches for his acrylic mother, the only
sound the low moan of *oxen.*
    The scene is set
to a hidden metronome,
I gather—thirty beats per minute—
rum pa pum pum—for you see,
I am the marker of time—the dark watcher
who warms her hands over nativities
in motion, drawn to their faint heat,
their geared cadence,
the advent synchronized,
the return of *oxen.*

RYAN HARPER

PILGRIMS

DEVIN MURPHY

Coulter felt wiggling fat rolls bunch from his waistline to clavicles as he pedaled up the long incline. A slow heat burned from his quads to the bone with each strained pump of his legs. *Top of the rise* had been his mantra for the last half hour on the hill. He'd rest at the top. He'd make it to the top. His jersey, frothed in sweat, stuck to his chest. His chest jiggled, and the bloom of embarrassment made him pump his legs harder. When he crested the hill he saw the long red and brown roll of Wyoming topography stretching out beneath a perfect blue sky. The sun glinted off the deep draws and rounded stones of dried creek beds on his glide down. With the wind whistling through his helmet and panniers, he was close to the feeling he had come for, of being healthy.

"I don't know why I miss that landscape," he'd told a friend before leaving. "I just do."

Now that he was in the West, away from everything he had built around him and called a life, he still couldn't describe it. The unassailable purity of the blue sky gave him a peace he had longed for, had known he had been missing for years. One truth was that he had become a soft, pink mess of a forty-five-year-old, overweight, pre-diabetic. Another, the one that mattered here, was that he felt very much at home flying downhill into the wind, and he was close to rediscovering some inner fire that used to drive him.

Several more large hills. Two he had to stop and push his bike on. Three long, fun descents. Then he found himself pedaling through rolling granite terraces that stretched out of sight. By his map, there was a town called Natrona, ten miles ahead.

He ate a tortilla wrap full of peanut butter and drank a pint of water.

When he reached the sign, it said, Natrona, Population 16, and all he saw was a train depot with a rusted diesel locomotive and a square, timber building with lacquered horizontal boarding and a neon-red Budweiser sign. There was no name on the bar. In the gravel lot were two pickup trucks with souped-up suspensions and tires and a military-green heavy truck.

When he walked in the bottom of his bike shoes click-clacked against the olive-green, faux-marble floor. A distorted mirror panel rose above the shelf with glasses, and the warped reflection made Coulter's eyes water. Two older men, each with blue mesh baseball caps curved in tight at the corners, sat at the far end of the bar. The men wore faded denim bib and brace overalls. A frumpy woman with teased auburn bangs, wide-waisted dickey blue slacks, and a V-neck T-shirt that showed off the top of her enormous, low-slung breasts, stood behind the counter. Coulter sat on a stool. The cracked leather felt hard against his sweaty bike shorts. His bike clips clanked against the foot rail.

"Hello," he said.

The three people didn't turn toward him.

In his spandex suit and tight, neon green jersey, his gray hair helmet-molded to his scalp, and the clip-clop of a rotund Baryshnikov, he was surprised they weren't staring at him.

"Excuse me, Ma'am," Coulter said, raising a finger to the bar.

The woman didn't look away from the two men. None of them were talking.

"Excuse me," Coulter said again.

She turned and walked toward him. Her reflection curved and swelled as she walked the length of the mirror.

He wanted to order a cold beer, a six-pack of cold beers, but he knew that was Fat Coulter talking, Fat Coulter craving calories he burned over the last three days of biking. "May I please have a water and a can of tomato juice?" He even hated his order.

"We don't have tomato juice."

"That there will do fine," Coulter pointed to the little cans of tomato juice next to the chrome coffee urn behind the counter.

"We don't have tomato juice," the woman said again. Her eyes were pinched, and even in the dim light, Coulter could see the shadow of a sickness beneath her skin. Cancer. ALS. Scurvy, for all he knew, as her lips didn't part when she spoke.

"Well. Do you serve any food?"

The two men at the end of the bar were looking at him now. Hard faces. One mustached, the other lined with deep-set wrinkles brimming with salt-and-pepper stubble along the jawline.

"Register's broken," she said. Light from the red bud sign found little puffs of space in her hair and swirled there as she shifted in front of Coulter.

"Well, can I pay for anything in this fine establishment?"

"There's a little shop a few miles up the road you can spend money at."

The men at the end of the bar were unflinching. The woman's gaze sharpened.

"A few miles up is all," she said. Her lips stayed locked together.

"I have cash."

"Just a few miles."

He eyed the funhouse mirror image of the bar, these out-of-the-way people, and the twisted version of himself.

"Well. Thanks for the hospitality," Coulter said, suppressing his urge to demand a bag of chips from behind the counter and yell, You're a bunch of cracked-brained yokels.

He eyed the funhouse mirror image of the bar, these out-of-the-way people, and the twisted version of himself. He liked what he saw, this other version of himself. At all other moments of his life, he would have turned and walked from the bar. He could see himself doing it and it made him angry. That was what fat Coulter who ate three candy bars a day would do and he knew it. So he pulled a cellphone from the jersey's zipper pocket at the small of his back. There were no reception bars. There had been none all day. He tapped the phone on the bar and pretended to dial. He made a show of putting it to his ear.

"Yeah, Allan. Yeah, it's me," he said to no one. He kept his eyes locked on the three people in the bar. Do it, he urged himself. "I'm at that dump you told me about in Natrona.

All three of the strangers turned toward him now.

He paused, surprised by what he was doing. But he liked the oddity of the moment and knowing that in these wide open spaces there was still room for him to be a different person. Not only change his body but how he acted.

"Yeah. The place is crawling with mice like you said. Just go ahead and file your report with the state inspector." Coulter grinned at the closed-mouth bartender. "Okay. Bye." He clicked the phone shut, pealed his wet bottom from the seat, eyed the two wet crescents of sweat left behind, and walked out.

In the parking lot his heart was a thumping knot. He sat by his bike for a moment and let his nerves settle. He'd surprised himself and was happy to have done so. As an act of owning what he had just done, he didn't start peddling away. He stood where he was and ate another peanut butter burrito, washed it down with a pint of water, then sat back on his bike. His undercarriage was raw and sore from where the seat pressed into his bottom. He started biking further north. The road was lined with meadow foxtail and white clover.

At any moment he expected a truck to come up the road and run him down.

Three miles from the yokel bar he rode with the noon time sun into a valley with a large gable-roofed house, a corrugated sheet barn, and a flat-roofed building with a sign painted on the side that said, bookstore. When he got closer there was a split rail fence running the length of the property with a posted a sign on every third post.

Because he'd felt good about what he'd done at the bar, and the idea of not being such a rule follower could crack a day open in new and interesting ways he rode onto the gravel driveway and leaned his bike against the fence and began walking up toward the house. The bookstore building was locked.

"Didn't hear anyone pull up," a woman's voice said behind him. She wore wire-rimmed glasses and paint-stained denim smock. "I can open that for you if you like."

"Oh, hello there. I don't want to trouble you. I thought I'd take a breather."

"No trouble," she said. "You on a pedal bike?"

"Yes. At least until I get run over."

"Well, that's impressive. Don't get many of you. Or, any of you, to be honest."

She pulled a key from her pocket and worked it into the lock. When the door swung open she hit a light and the inside was full of bookshelves, each almost seven feet tall, and two books deep on musty shelves that bowed under the weight.

"Whoa," Coulter said. The musty scent and old joy of book stacks settled over him. He'd spent a lifetime voraciously reading for decades, and this room was a random gift laid in his lap. "This is unexpected."

"I guess it is."

The first shelf he looked at was full of coffee table books of famous painters. The next shelf had French novels. Down the line were contemporary poetry, gardening, political and law books, anthropology, psychology, and row after row of what seemed to be a random scatter of fiction and nonfiction. There was a reference shelf. He scanned the spines. One was, *Living With Diabetes.* He let his finger touch upon it but moved away from the shelf.

"This collection is amazing."

"Thank you."

"How can you keep a book store way out here?"

"Mostly just for our own use. Though we like the idea of running a book store. Which is funny, because we almost never open it. People drive up, see the door shut, and turn around. Happens I heard your feet on the gravel and took a look."

"I'm glad you did. This place is heaven."

"Glad you like it. You a book lover?"

"Yes. For my whole life." Coulter was eager to talk to this woman. He had been eager to talk to someone in the bar down the road, too. "Too much time sitting and reading," he said and slapped his open palms hard against his gut. There was some truth to that. He'd been a poor eater most of his life. Food as a crutch, he'd been told. He'd been a nervous kid and it carried over. Afraid of his father and then to let anyone close enough to hold such sway over him. He cloistered himself with books and snacks.

"Well, you feel free to look around as much as you like. Yell up to the house if I can help you with anything."

"You don't mind leaving me here?"

"Well, it doesn't seem like you can get very far with very much, to be honest, so you're welcome to park it as long as you like."

"Awfully nice of you. Thank you."

"You're welcome." She walked out and left Coulter with the books. He knew he should keep biking, keep burning calories, but instead wandered among the books.

In the back of the room was a yellow sheet for a curtain that he pushed aside and found a low-ceilinged room with no windows. There were white plaster walls, lined with bookshelves of antique, leather-bound books. There was a hand-written journal starting from 1762 of a man named Jacque La Véredrye who was exploring Alberta and living among the native tribes of the plains. He had drawn pictures of the village and faces of the people he lived with. He recorded their day-to-day lives. He wrote about his own life as the son of a French-Canadian trapper who trained him to come to the mountains of the West, but with his immediate fascination with what and who he found on the plains, he wanted to capture the essence of the lives of natives instead of taking anything from the land.

Coulter read well into the first volume of the notes.

Hours passed. After half a day of reading he felt like he had known this author his whole life. As he read this other man's histories he felt something inside of him emerging from a chrysalis. He imagined himself as an early explorer on the Alberta plains, not this man bending towards fat, who had set up a life far from great fields of wildflowers.

Books held his connection to the world, and it was exciting to find this spirit laid down on parchment in the middle of an odd and lonely state...

He knew this was not how most people came to know others. But to him, learning was holy, and it happened in the quiet of pages laid one after the other, volume after volume, year after year. Books held his connection to the world, and it was exciting to find this spirit laid down on parchment in the middle of an odd and lonely state in the West.

He had gotten lost in books like this before and it was when he felt the most alive.

Coulter sold medical supplies and traveled around the Midwest all week. He spent his nights reading in hotel rooms. His father was a philosophy professor and Coulter had taken over two thousand books from his house after he died. Coulter wanted to keep them and get to know his father to see what his father was looking for in all those texts. Coulter found the text dry, too abstract in their arguments and thinking, but his father's margin notes, often in the red marker he used to grade, often messy to read, were fascinating. There was forty years of the man's thoughts, his inner life, that Coulter stored for a while, but there was a water damage issue, and most were ruined outright or lost to the mold that ensued. All that red ink blurred. His father's lifetime of thoughts bled away.

That was why now, with the leather-bound journal, he felt an inner life laid out for him to explore and know. It was exciting and sad, remembering his father's lost work, the man quietly taking time with his books, probably tired from teaching and raising Coulter. He admired his father for his unending reflection and questioning of the world—probing himself as well, a skill Coulter was only now coming to employ.

Coulter did not know how many hours had passed when he heard the woman call out. "Hello. Are you still here?"

"Hi. I'm back here." He started to shuffle to his feet but his legs locked up.

The woman stood in the doorway at the curtain.

"Sorry. I got caught up back here. These books are wonderful."

"The same things happens to me. It's getting late, and you're a bit of a way from anywhere."

"That's okay. I'm camping, so I can pull onto a field up ahead."

"You're welcome to camp on our land for the night, if you wish."

"That's kind of you. I'd really appreciate that."

"No problem. I'm Holly."

"Coulter."

"Let me show you around, Coulter."

Coulter was hesitant to put down the Alberta journals of Jacque La Véredry.

Holly led him to the back of the house. She pointed to a wide field stretching to a small rise with a jagged boulder ridge to the east.

"The stars are right on top of you back here. You can bring your bike around and use the field for your campsite."

Coulter brought his bike around, pitched his bivy sack tent, and changed from his biking clothes to a pair of light weight shorts, a T-shirt, and sandals. He heated up a package of noodles on his Coleman stove and ate the last of the peanut butter burritos he'd made that morning. He wanted a candy bar. Sugar of any kind. He'd been addicted to it for years and with every gas station in the country full of rainbow racks of it, it was easy. Now he was trying to pedal free of it before it warped his body beyond repair.

When he'd eaten, the sun was beginning to dip in the west. He walked to the house to ask if he could fill his water bottles.

"This must be our wandering bard," a middle-aged blond woman in a green short-sleeved, V-neck jumper said.

"I guess that's me. I spoke with Holly earlier. I'm Coulter."

"Coulter. I'm Katherine, Holly's wife."

"Nice to meet you Katherine. Mind if I fill up my water bottles?"

"Not at all, I can even top the offer of tap water if you'd like to share a glass of wine."

"I'd love that," Coulter said, dismissing the new voice of the calorie and sugar intake counter.

Coulter and Katherine sat in a wicker chair on the veranda of the wrap around porch, each drinking a glass of cold white wine and watching the sunset. Holly came and sat with them with her own glass and a new bottle of wine. Her free hand reached out, and she dragged a fingertip across her wife's knuckles. Coulter was drawn to these women, struck right away by the ease with each other in such a wide-open domain, and he envied their living where they did, their having each other.

They talked and drank. The women were both lawyers from Kansas City who wanted to get as far away from the bustle of their careers as they could, and bought the ranch property seven years before and spent their days reveling in their privacy.

"Now I feel bad for butting into your haven," Coulter said.

"I find the wonder you have in our books engaging," Holly said. "Besides, we need some visitors from time to time."

They drank the second bottle and started on a third as it was getting dark. It took its time getting dark there.

The women spoke of their lives in Wyoming. They had two extra generators and two meat freezers full of processed elk with select cuts wrapped in brown butcher paper which helped them get through the bad Chinook storms. They talked of where they came from, their work lives.

"What do you do here?" Coulter asked.

"We paint," Katherine said.

"What do you do when you're not painting?"

Coulter was drawn to these women, struck right away by the ease with each other in such a wide-open domain...

"Talk about painting," Holly jumped in.

Then Coulter began asking about the books and how they came upon the leather-bound frontier journals.

"Nothing special, I'm afraid," Holly said. "Just an estate sale in Jackson Hole. Not sure how they traveled before that. Not really sure if they're worth much or not."

They kept talking and drinking wine, and it seemed his hosts were as eager for the company as he was. They asked about his bike route, the logistics, and if he'd taken other trips like this."

He hadn't. This was a once-in-a-lifetime adventure he'd dreamed of and finally taken when he found out he was becoming sick and feared his life was about to turn stale and start to sour.

They told him of trips they'd taken. "We went this last spring to Kearny, Nebraska, to see the sand cranes migrate," Holly said.

"That is a sight," Katherine agreed, "but it happens when the weather is awful."

"We drove down there and went before the sun came up to sit in a lean-to to watch them by the river," Holly said.

"They dance with each other," Katherine said.

"How so?" Coulter asked.

"Well, it's hard to describe," Holly said. She pushed back her chair and started moving around in a circle, as a corkscrew digging through the deck until she was coiled with bent knees. She sprung upward, leapt off the ground higher than he would have guessed her age would allow, her arms shot outward, fingers fanned out, knuckles taught, and for a minute she was frozen in mid-jump. Levitating. She landed and jumped again, as if never touching the deck. Her neck, delicate and white, elongated, and her ponytail swayed from shoulder to shoulder.

"And they sing," Katherine said.

"How do they sing?"

Holly kept jumping.

Katherine started making bird songs that sounded like a piercing wind pushing through a canyon.

Even as it was happening, Coulter knew he would remember these two women dancing and doing bird calls for the rest of his days. Watching them he felt the troll of his own loneliness that clung to his back and kept him beneath the currents of living with and loving others.

When they said goodnight, Coulter walked out to the field to his tent. He leapt and spun several times, imitating Holly imitating a crane. He was happy and full of energy despite his sore legs and rear. He would ask to read more of the journals in the morning, perhaps make arrangements to buy them and have them shipped home. Jacque La Véredrye could travel back before he did. He liked the idea of the journals on the move again. He had to keep pedaling for the sake of shaking off the rust he felt lining any sense of love of wider world he had as a young man. His father had wanted to be left alone with his work, but in his place he delivered Melville, London, and Hemmingway. Paper adventures for a young boy. Now he had to pedal into his own adventure until he no longer jiggled and felt that shame of not controlling his own body any longer.

Instead of sleeping he took a flashlight and wandered up the hill in order to get even closer to the white pulse and heartbeat of the stars as they came out. When he reached the boulders, he climbed over a few and came to the top of the rise. There he looked east and saw what looked like a string of stars resting on the ground. A runway to the past. When he focused his eyes, he realized they were a long line of lantern lights. Tents and campfires stretched out into the east and what must have been hundreds of people walking across the nowhere landscape toward the hill he stood on. Coulter stood watching for a minute, unsure if he was drunker than he thought or if the fun-house mirror in Natrona had blurred his vision. He climbed down the rocks and ran across the field back to the deck where Katherine and Holly holding hands and sipping wine.

"Maybe I'm going crazy, but it looks like a thousand people are hiking up to your property over that hill."

"Mormons," Holly said. "You know how I told you we moved to the middle of nowhere to get away from people, especially judgmental people? Well, we didn't think to ask if this ranch was smack on the Mormon Trail."

"You're kidding?"

"Nope. Every summer, thousands of them come marching along. That's why we've got all those posted signs on our ranch."

"They're going to Utah. Mormon pilgrims by the millions. An endless procession of them. They come bearing down on us and then loop around, because we put up such a stink, and they didn't quite want to deal with a pair of pussy-baring, pussy-loving lawyers."

"That's the damndest thing."

"You're telling us," Holly said.

Coulter walked back to his tent, climbed the hill again and looked down on the Mormon pilgrims.

God, he loved the west. The air, the land changing from stark to beautiful along every line on a map, and the endless versions of people filling their days. He loved how he could reinvent himself a little at a time every day and no one would notice or care. He could bike around from one ready adventure to the next until he finally found a version of himself that he could love. ■

IN MY WINDOW

A cloud in a cup.

My diary with its flimsy metal lock.

Milky sheets of winter plastic to keep in the heat.

Mother has wedged father's drumsticks into the top rail of every window frame—her alarm system while he's away. Father speaks all over Tennessee in chalk-dusted lecture halls about phyla, kingdoms, families, and orders. Demognathus Ochrophaeus is tendered to the rock of a creek bed. Plethodon Aureolis prefers the scent of its own.

These nights our mother orders take-out from Shirley's. Eggs and bacon appear at our door in a Styrofoam box.

She arranges her African violets by the wood stove, gives me cement-colored sticks of plant food to push into the soil.

Out the window, my brother walks to the shed for more tender. He has a woodpecker feather in the bill of his cap and the shadow of hair above his lip.

Sometimes, out the window, I see lost beagles returning to us with blood-bristled fur. And at the end of the day, coywolves circling the driveway while we lie in our beds, their yellow eyes glowing green in the moon-swollen night.

Out the window are the places where the deer go to die, the hollows where we find their bones smooth and cool as cream.

In the mornings I see the two trees with bicycle locks clipped around them; those belong to me. There is the hill where father shot the kitten—already dying when it was born, and the barn where I listened for the percussion with my head under my jacket.

Out the window the black well-water lines connected by metal cuppings run to the spring. I follow the lines with my brother when things freeze. How I wish to find in winter the burst of holly berries in the snow, the fire inside a pinecone, spring peepers hardened in the leaf litter.

Father has promised to return with the giant Christmas stocking that hangs in the IGA window. Every afternoon, I watch for the hood of his blue Taurus to come around the bend of our driveway, but there is only cold gravel and the brown scrub of dead grass.

There is only our sloping yard leading to the woods, only a view of branches and sky tossing in a white-painted frames; creek water loosens and flows again under the ice; trout wait in muddy holes with their gills puffing in and out.

In the treetops, birds of the day become stars at night.

LYDIA COPELAND GWYN

POWER OUTAGE

somewhere wind or lightning licks a swooning tree
somewhere the line drags sparks like a dangling muffler

here I rest in the dreamless sleep
a panoramic depicting night minus walls windows door

the inverse of the *Eureka!* moment
stretches black for maybe hours

I can't see what I can't see & imagine what I can
as I search with dim-witted fingers

for a flashlight or sacred candle
a North Star guiding sailors in a drawer

ACE BOGGESS

BOOK REVIEW

Sarah Einstein. *Mot: A Memoir*. Athens, Ga.: University of Georgia Press, 2015. 168 pages. Hardcover. $24.95.

Reviewed by Greta McDonough

The story of *Mot* and its author, Sarah Einstein, might be unbelievable as a work of fiction, which makes this memoir all the more remarkable in its telling. Serving the story of an improbable friendship are elements, both big and small, that lend veracity to the storytelling and create in Einstein a reliable narrator.

From the memoir's opening in a KOA campground in a hard-luck part of Amarillo, Texas, the reader is hooked immediately by the lush description and the delicate foreshadowing of an unlikely pair of friends. Mot is a homeless drifter in his mid-sixties, who is waiting—or we think he is waiting—for Einstein's visit. She has driven from West Virginia, alone, to spend a platonic week with him, sharing a cabin and seeing the sights, leaving behind her new husband and step-daughter, and a marriage still straining from its brevity and the negotiations of merging several lives into one.

We know almost immediately that Mot is suffering from severe mental illness—the voices, the paranoia, and at times the word-salad of the truly disturbed—and that Einstein knows him as a former client from her stint at the Friendship Room, a drop-in day facility for the homeless and mentally ill. We are not sure what to make of Einstein, a woman on the verge of middle age, and Mot, who is in possession of voices and delusions and "The Big Guys Upstairs." Anyone with a passing understanding of mental health issues will see warnings and red flags, and from time to time the reader may feel a pang or two of discomfort. We wonder about the propriety of such a friendship, all the boundary business that is the cornerstone of working with vulnerable clients, and this wondering is echoed in the descriptions of a relationship that Einstein's husband has with his own client, Rita. But as the story unfolds, the narrator provides space for our questions while laying her story brick-by-brick in a subtle, elegant way.

We are not sure, early on, what motivates the narrator to pursue her friendship with Mot, who has left West Virginia. Einstein has vacated her position at the day center after a traumatic event. She packs up and leaves her husband for a week, something he supports in light of his own enmeshed relationship with a mentally ill client. We can't imagine how a friendship with Mot can be sustained or sustaining. But they are friends, enjoying each other's company, cooking together, swimming, and talking, although awkwardly at times, about all sorts of things. She likes his company. He fusses over the health of her car. Their excursions include many trips to

Pep Boys and AutoZone so he can keep her Toyota in prime condition. We think, in this small gesture, that he worries about her, cares for her. That he is her friend. She enjoys her time with him, but wonders, too, about this "fragile faith" she has in him. Is he safe? With her? Around children? Is this foolish, her effort with this man?

By the end of this enlightening and engaging read, many of the reader's questions are answered. Through an economic and tightly structured book, we begin to understand mental illness in a new, more human way—not a clinical discussion, but the day-to-day reality of it, told from a loving and practical point of view.

Mot gives the reader a glimpse into the world of the truly disenfranchised, especially the invisible world of the homeless. With an economy of language but sharp detail, Einstein shows us the reality of living "off the grid." She describes Mot sleeping behind abandoned buildings and in Walmart parking lots after he buys a beat-up car. She gives the reader a glimpse of the homeless person's day, showing us how Mot, upon rising each morning, gathers his meager belongings and hides them somewhere safe to be retrieved later. He then cruises the aisles of Walmart, charging his phone in the small appliances department. For anyone who has worked with or knows someone who is homeless, these small details ground the story in reality and ring true. For those who have not had this experience, these elements provide a glimpse into this hidden world. Einstein writes of Mot's struggles with mental illness, the voices, the one named Moloch who "lives" in his throat and who chokes Mot and alters his voice when he speaks. She describes with spare prose the way he lives, the way he leaves, here one day, gone tomorrow, and the mechanisms by which he stays connected, at least tenuously, with the real world. We see his world as chaotic. But the writing is anything but. In fact, it is through seamless prose, word choice, and imagery that the reader comes to understand Mot's chaos and accept it, just as Einstein does.

In both the memoir's title and in an interview with *Brevity*, Einstein admits that she has written a memoir in which the narrator isn't the main character. That she is telling Mot's story. But of course, in doing so, she is also telling her own, which unfolds on a canvas strewn with Walmarts, campgrounds, and a home life that is fractured, loving, and supportive in equal measures. We like the time we spend with Mot and Einstein. We understand them better by book's end. We understand the world a bit better, too, and perhaps, ourselves. ■

Adrian Blevins & Karen Salyer McElmurray, Eds. *Walk Till the Dogs Get Mean: Meditations on the Forbidden from Contemporary Appalachia*. Athens, Ohio: Ohio University Press, 2015. 288 pages. Softcover. $26.95.

Reviewed by Beth Newberry

The anthology *Walk Till The Dogs Get Mean: Meditations of the Forbidden from Contemporary Appalachia*, edited by Adrian Blevins and Karen Salyer McElmurray, is a canonizing collection of creative nonfiction that gathers the experiences of thirty-two writers to reveal many aspects of the forbidden with Appalachian cultures of the last seventy-five years. The topics include a coming to terms with sexual identity, transgender identity, race, politics, individual expression of self, how pursuing individual dreams within communal responsibilities, among others, within the context of being Appalachian. In this collective act of the challenging the silence of the forbidden, the editors are attempting to answer,

"Weren't we ourselves—full-blown Appalachians?...Why are we excluding ourselves from our own canon?"

The anthology as a whole makes transparent the mutual and often painful experience of being from a place that is home but that cannot be home forever because of the confines of culture, family or geography. Each essay exposes the struggle of going off from home and the longing and loneliness—or alternately the comfort and celebration—that the journey and distance brings.

This collection offers nonfiction accounts of established, contemporary Appalachian writers as well as emerging ones. Recognizable voices from the Appalachian literary cannon include Chris Offutt, bell hooks, Silas House, Dorothy Allison, and Crystal Wilkinson. Emerging artists include the likes of Jessie van Eerden, whose essay contributes the title to the collection. Her essay "Walk Till the Dogs Get Mean," is a gracefully constructed and meditative personal essay about her return to West Virginia and reconstructing her life after the end of her marriage. In a search for peace and what comes next, the narrator walks the hills and neighborhood of her home and also tries to write her way through the pain, writing on scraps of paper "Walk till the dogs get mean and then walk a little further."

Van Eerden follows her own directives, both literal and figurative, as she walks herself toward healing: "I notice among them is the basic truth the mean dogs know of the world: hunger and waves of animal hurt...I see there's... something inside the hunger; it's like glimpsing the soft pink scar-skin where this one husky has lost its ear." All the dogs she encounters also nudge her to confront her own feelings.

"Homesick for what? For something older than myself, something ancient and inside hunger and inside sickbed loneliness and inside a tending and inside a song; home is inside-of and also holding it all."

In other sections of the anthology, the forbidden comes in many forms, whether with religion, gender identity or race. In "Homeless" by Michael Croley, the author recounts his coming to terms with the validity of his life as material for his creative writing. "When my fiction writing professor learned that I was half-Korean and from Appalachia she wondered why I wasn't writing about that," begins his piece. Interspersed with the story of his education as a young writer are two other stories: one of his mother's migration to Corbin, Kentucky at the age of nineteen with her husband, Croley's father, from Korea, and the second is a historic and personal history of his hometown of Corbin.

The essay is more of a critical one with lyrical notes and thoughtful structure—interspersing passages that are plainly told with carefully chosen details. Croley depicts the town as a character in his past with details such as Corbin being the home to the first KFC, detailing how the railway system shaped the town, and the town's history of racism—the expulsion of its African American citizens in 1919. These historical facts are offset with stories of the writer's childhood and young adult life:

> *I was called Ching-Chong, a Japanese motherfucker, a Chinese motherfucker, and a Chink. During an argument with a female classmate, she hatefully said to me, "Why don't you just go back to where you came from?" And I replied, knowing full well how this would spite her, "You mean, up the road?"*

So "Homesick for what?" is a question Croley has to answer as he embraces his mother's story and his own as not one that is forbidden to tell, but one that is essential to his purpose as a writer. And as with each piece in *Walk Till the Dogs Get Mean*, the veil is lifted on what is forbidden when silence is ended. This collection reveals an essential nature of being an Appalachian writer—that what has not been said is often the most important thing to say. ■

TO KNOW A MAN TRULY,

know the music that comes with him,
the way he talks, his food,
and the way his ear curls on his jaw.
Know the light in his eyes, as
the light he lives in.

Though you are gone, I still hear
the music of your country.
It slams around through the trees
and the creeks and lies
on the porch with its heart beating fast.

NOEL SMITH

KEEPSAKE

On the famous path by the river,
I stoop and pick up a Buckeye
To keep in my pocket.

It is mine this river as it flows past
your house which is also mine, flows
past

its banks of paw paws
and cowcumber trees, with their nodding
saucer leaves.

The river's riffles
froth by the shoal before they run
full out, gurgling their

pebbly songs. You have
taken the tune out of them and gone.
I have this Buckeye.

NOEL SMITH

UNITED STATES POSTAL SERVICE®

Statement of Ownership, Management, and Circulation (All Periodicals Publications Except Requester Publications)

1. Publication Title	2. Publication Number	3. Filing Date
Appalachian Heritage	0 3 6 3 – 2 8 1 8	September 23, 2015

4. Issue Frequency	5. Number of Issues Published Annually	6. Annual Subscription Price
Quarterly (Winter, Spring, Summer, Fall)	4	$30 individual $40 institution

7. Complete Mailing Address of Known Office of Publication (*Not printer*) (*Street, city, county, state, and ZIP+4®*)

The Loyal Jones Appalachian Center, CPO Box 2166,
Berea College, Madison County, Berea, KY 40404

Contact Person: Suzi Waters

Telephone (*Include area code*): 919--962--4201

8. Complete Mailing Address of Headquarters or General Business Office of Publisher (*Not printer*)

The University of North Carolina Press, 116 South Boundary St, Chapel Hill, Orange County, NC 27514

9. Full Names and Complete Mailing Addresses of Publisher, Editor, and Managing Editor (*Do not leave blank*)

Publisher (*Name and complete mailing address*)

The University of North Carolina Press, 116 South Boundary St, Chapel Hill, Orange County, NC 27514

Editor (*Name and complete mailing address*)

Jason K. Howard, The Loyal Jones Appalachian Center, CPO Box 2166, Berea College, Madison County, Berea, KY 40404

Managing Editor (*Name and complete mailing address*)

same as above editor

10. Owner (*Do not leave blank. If the publication is owned by a corporation, give the name and address of the corporation immediately followed by the names and addresses of all stockholders owning or holding 1 percent or more of the total amount of stock. If not owned by a corporation, give the names and addresses of the individual owners. If owned by a partnership or other unincorporated firm, give its name and address as well as those of each individual owner. If the publication is published by a nonprofit organization, give its name and address.*)

Full Name	Complete Mailing Address
The Loyal Jones Appalachian Center	CPO Box 2166, 205 North Main St, Berea, KY 40404

11. Known Bondholders, Mortgagees, and Other Security Holders Owning or Holding 1 Percent or More of Total Amount of Bonds, Mortgages, or Other Securities. If none, check box → ☒ None

Full Name	Complete Mailing Address

12. Tax Status (*For completion by nonprofit organizations authorized to mail at nonprofit rates*) (*Check one*)
The purpose, function, and nonprofit status of this organization and the exempt status for federal income tax purposes:
☒ Has Not Changed During Preceding 12 Months
☐ Has Changed During Preceding 12 Months (*Publisher must submit explanation of change with this statement*)

PS Form **3526**, July 2014 (*Page 1 of 4 (see instructions page 4)*) PSN: 7530-01-000-9931 **PRIVACY NOTICE:** See our privacy policy on www.usps.com

13. Publication Title	14. Issue Date for Circulation Data Below
Appalachian Heritage	Summer 2015 43#3 Sept.22,'15

15. Extent and Nature of Circulation			Average No. Copies Each Issue During Preceding 12 Months	No. Copies of Single Issue Published Nearest to Filing Date
a. Total Number of Copies *(Net press run)*			1000	1000
b. Paid Circulation *(By Mail and Outside the Mail)*	(1)	Mailed Outside-County Paid Subscriptions Stated on PS Form 3541 (Include paid distribution above nominal rate, advertiser's proof copies, and exchange copies)	412	420
	(2)	Mailed In-County Paid Subscriptions Stated on PS Form 3541 *(Include paid distribution above nominal rate, advertiser's proof copies, and exchange copies)*		
	(3)	Paid Distribution Outside the Mails Including Sales Through Dealers and Carriers, Street Vendors, Counter Sales, and Other Paid Distribution Outside USPS®		
	(4)	Paid Distribution by Other Classes of Mail Through the USPS (e.g., First-Class Mail®)		
c. Total Paid Distribution *[Sum of 15b (1), (2), (3), and (4)]* ▶			412	420
d. Free or Nominal Rate Distribution *(By Mail and Outside the Mail)*	(1)	Free or Nominal Rate Outside-County Copies included on PS Form 3541	63	77
	(2)	Free or Nominal Rate In-County Copies Included on PS Form 3541		
	(3)	Free or Nominal Rate Copies Mailed at Other Classes Through the USPS (e.g., First-Class Mail)		
	(4)	Free or Nominal Rate Distribution Outside the Mail *(Carriers or other means)*		
e. Total Free or Nominal Rate Distribution *(Sum of 15d (1), (2), (3) and (4))*			63	77
f. Total Distribution *(Sum of 15c and 15e)* ▶			475	497
g. Copies not Distributed *(See Instructions to Publishers #4 (page #3))* ▶			525	503
h. Total *(Sum of 15f and g)*			1000	1000
i. Percent Paid *(15c divided by 15f times 100)* ▶			87%	85%

* If you are claiming electronic copies, go to line 16 on page 3. If you are not claiming electronic copies, skip to line 17 on page 3.

17. Publication of Statement of Ownership

☒ If the publication is a general publication, publication of this statement is required. Will be printed in the Fall 2015 issue of this publication. ☐ Publication not required.

18. Signature and Title of Editor, Publisher, Business Manager, or Owner	Date
Robert Durcho[illegible] CFO, USC PRESS	9/22/2015

I certify that all information furnished on this form is true and complete. I understand that anyone who furnishes false or misleading information on this form or who omits material or information requested on the form may be subject to criminal sanctions (including fines and imprisonment) and/or civil sanctions (including civil penalties).

PS Form **3526**, July 2014

CONTRIBUTORS

Ace Boggess is the author of two books of poetry: *The Prisoners* (Brick Road Poetry Press, 2014) and *The Beautiful Girl Whose Wish Was Not Fulfilled* (Highwire Press, 2003). He is an ex-con, ex-husband, ex-reporter, and completely exhausted by all the things he isn't anymore. His writing has appeared in *Harvard Review, Mid-American Review, RATTLE, River Styx, North Dakota Quarterly,* and many other journals. He lives in Charleston, West Virginia.

Kathleen Driskell is associate editor of the *Louisville Review* and professor of creative writing at Spalding University, where she also helps direct the low-residency MFA in writing. She is the author of numerous books and collections, including *Next Door to the Dead* and *Seed Across Snow.*

Amelia Fowler lives in West Virginia. She writes about outer space and mental illness. Her essay "Space and Time" was included as a notable in *Best American Essays 2015.*

Lydia Copeland Gwyn's work has appeared or is forthcoming in the *Florida Review, NANO Fiction, New World Writing, Elm Leaves Journal, Glimmer Train,* and other publications. Her flash fiction manuscript, *In the Air a Shining Heart,* won second place in the *Florida Review*'s Jeanne Leiby Memorial Chapbook Award. She lives in East Tennessee with her husband, son, and daughter.

Richard Hague's prose has appeared in his collections *Milltown Natural: Essays & Stories From a Life, Learning How: Stories, Yarns, & Tales*; and *Lives of the Poem: Community & Connection in a Writing Life,* as well as in *Creative Nonfiction, Appalachian Journal, Now & Then, Pine Mountain Sand & Gravel,* and several anthologies. He received the 2012 Weatherford Award in Poetry. He lives, writes, and operates a small urban farm in Cincinnati.

Ryan Harper is a visiting assistant professor in the Department of Religion and Philosophy at Presbyterian College in South Carolina. Recent work has appeared or is forthcoming in *Adanna, Still,*

Berkeley Poetry Review, Killing the Buddha, and elsewhere. His poetry chapbook, *Memphis Left at Cairo* (2013) is available through Finishing Line Press, and his ethnography of southern gospel music will be available through the University Press of Mississippi in 2016.

Carol Hobbs is a poet from Newfoundland where the Appalachian Mountain Range extends north to the Long Range Mountains. She lives, writes, and teaches high school English and creative writing in Hudson, Massachusetts. Her work has appeared in journals, magazines, and anthologies in Canada, Ireland, and the United States of America. Her book manuscript, *New Found Lande*, received a New England PEN Discovery Prize.

Maurice Manning's most recent books are *The Gone and the Going Away*, his fifth collection of poems, and *The Rag-Picker's Guide to Poetry*, co-edited with Eleanor Wilner. A former Guggenheim Fellow, Manning has been a finalist for the Pulitzer Prize and is a member of The Fellowship of Southern Writers. He teaches at Transylvania University and in the MFA Program for Writers at Warren Wilson College.

Tessa McCoy is a senior communications major at the University of Virginia's College at Wise. Her poetry has appeared in *Still: The Journal* and *Jimson Weed*, and her short story "I Can Get Someone on Register 3" won the first *Jimson Weed* writing contest. She is currently the chief managing editor of *Jimson Weed*, a literary publication of The University of Virginia's College at Wise.

Greta McDonough is the author of *Her Troublesome Boys: The Lucy Furman Story*. She has written several award-winning essays and her work has appeared in *Still: The Journal, Now and Then, Kentucky Living, Kentucky Monthly*, and regional news publications. She teaches social work and writes in Owensboro, Kentucky.

Jeremy S. McQueen is the author of the essay and poetry collection *Pillow Talk Confessions*. An excerpt from McQueen's unpublished novel, *Nights on Fire*, appeared in the Fall 2015 issue of *Still: The Journal*. He earned his Bachelor of Arts degree from Berea College and his Master of Science degree from Eastern Kentucky University. He lives on Solar Place Farm in Somerset, Kentucky.

Jennifer Even Melton is a professional writer and editor and a native New Englander who now calls London, Kentucky, her home. Her photographs reflect her passion for the wonder of being.

Devin Murphy's recent fiction appears in *The Chicago Tribune, Glimmer Train, The Michigan Quarterly Review, The Missouri Review,* and *Shenandoah,* as well as over fifty other literary journals and anthologies. He holds an MFA from Colorado State University, a Creative Writing PhD from the University of Nebraska-Lincoln, and is now an Assistant Professor of Creative Writing at Bradley University.

Paul Nelson's latest of eight books is *Burning the Furniture* (Guernica Editions, 2014). His work has won an AWP Award for Poetry, a University of Alabama Press Series Selection, and an NEA Fellowship. For a decade, he was Professor and Director of Creative Writing at Ohio University, and he lives and writes now on the North Shore of O'ahu, though he is by life a Maine Downeaster.

Beth Newberry is a writer and editor living in Louisville, Kentucky. Her work has been published in *Sojourners, Still: The Journal,* and *The Louisville Review.* Her essay "The Center of the Compass" was named a notable essay of 2010 by Robert Atwan in the 2011 *Best American Essays.* She writes at thehillville.com.

Noel Smith spent several years in Leslie County, Kentucky, as a social worker for the Frontier Nursing Service in the 1950s and 1960s, sometimes visiting her clients on horseback. A native New Yorker, she returned home where she taught elementary school. Her poetry collection *The Well String* (MotesBooks, 2008) is a collection of narrative poems about the people she knew while in Kentucky. She now lives in the lower Hudson Valley of New York.

Terry Ann Thaxton has published two full-length collections: *Getaway Girl* and *The Terrible Wife,* as well as a textbook, *Creative Writing in the Community: A Guide.* She has published essays and poetry in *Connecticut Review, Defunct, Gulf Coast, Cimarron Review,* and other journals. She holds an MFA from Vermont College of Fine Arts and teaches creative writing at the University of Central Florida, where she also directs the MFA program.